ARROYO CENTER

Resources Required to Meet the U.S. Army's Enlisted Recruiting Requirements Under Alternative Recruiting Goals, Conditions, and Eligibility Policies

David Knapp, Bruce R. Orvis, Christopher E. Maerzluft, Tiffany Tsai

Prepared for the United States Army

Approved for public release; distribution unlimited

For more information on this publication, visit www.rand.org/t/RR2364

Library of Congress Cataloging-in-Publication Data is available for this publication.
ISBN: 978-1-9774-0020-8

Published by the RAND Corporation, Santa Monica, Calif.
© Copyright 2018 RAND Corporation
RAND® is a registered trademark.

Cover: Photo courtesy of U.S. Army Recruiting Command.

Limited Print and Electronic Distribution Rights

This document and trademark(s) contained herein are protected by law. This representation of RAND intellectual property is provided for noncommercial use only. Unauthorized posting of this publication online is prohibited. Permission is given to duplicate this document for personal use only, as long as it is unaltered and complete. Permission is required from RAND to reproduce, or reuse in another form, any of its research documents for commercial use. For information on reprint and linking permissions, please visit www.rand.org/pubs/permissions.

The RAND Corporation is a research organization that develops solutions to public policy challenges to help make communities throughout the world safer and more secure, healthier and more prosperous. RAND is nonprofit, nonpartisan, and committed to the public interest.

RAND's publications do not necessarily reflect the opinions of its research clients and sponsors.

Support RAND
Make a tax-deductible charitable contribution at
www.rand.org/giving/contribute

www.rand.org

Preface

This report documents research and analysis conducted as part of a project entitled *Resources Needed to Meet Army's Enlisted Accession Requirements*, sponsored by the Assistant Secretary of the Army for Manpower & Reserve Affairs. The purpose of the project was to enhance the effectiveness and efficiency of the Army's use of the suite of available recruiting resources and policies by optimizing the required resource levels and mix to support future recruiting under changing enlisted accession requirements, varying labor market conditions and recruiting environments, and alternative recruit eligibility policies, and by enabling the assessment of alternative courses of action.

The Project Unique Identification Code (PUIC) for the project that produced this document is HQD146830.

This research was conducted within RAND Arroyo Center's Personnel, Training, and Health Program. RAND Arroyo Center, part of the RAND Corporation, is a federally funded research and development center (FFRDC) sponsored by the United States Army.

RAND operates under a "Federal-Wide Assurance" (FWA00003425) and complies with the *Code of Federal Regulations for the Protection of Human Subjects Under United States Law* (45 CFR 46), also known as "the Common Rule," as well as with the implementation guidance set forth in DoD Instruction 3216.02. As applicable, this compliance includes reviews and approvals by RAND's Institutional Review Board (the Human Subjects Protection Committee) and by the U.S. Army. The views of sources utilized in this study are solely their own and do not represent the official policy or position of DoD or the U.S. government.

Table of Contents

Figures

Tables

Summary

The research described in this report is intended to enhance the effectiveness and efficiency of the Army's use of recruiting resources and enlistment eligibility policies by optimizing the required resource levels and mix to support future recruiting under changing enlisted accession requirements, varying labor market conditions and recruiting environments, and alternative recruit eligibility policies, and by enabling the assessment of alternative courses of action.

The Army spent on average $1.5 billion annually in 2016 dollars on recruiting resources (including recruiter compensation) from fiscal year (FY) 2001 to FY 2014, and nearly $2.0 billion annually in FY 2008 and FY 2009.[1] The variation in cost reflects differences in both the recruiting environment and the accession mission. Recruiting is a complex process, requiring enlistment contracts to be signed months in advance of the enlistee starting Basic Combat Training, and there is a nontrivial probability that enlistees will cancel their contracts during this time period. The resources used to produce additional contracts, such as recruiters, bonuses, and advertising, differ not only in their cost per additional contract produced but also in time elapsed between resource use and productive response. Additionally, the Army alters recruit eligibility policies to achieve its annual accession requirement. During difficult recruiting

---

[1] Recruiters, advertising, and enlistment bonuses offered to prospective recruits peaked in FY 2007–2008. Because bonuses are paid upon completion of Initial Entry Training (IET)—and for bonuses over $10,000, the remainder is paid out over the recruit's term of enlistment—the actual costs incurred by the Army peaked in FY 2008–2009.

environments, it has offered additional enlistment waivers, permitted more soldiers with prior service to enlist, and lowered educational and test score requirements.

Understanding how recruiting resources and enlistment eligibility policies work together as a system under varying recruiting requirements and environments is critical for decisionmakers who want to use their limited resources to efficiently and effectively achieve the Army's accession requirements. This research builds on earlier work by Defense Manpower Data Center researchers on the effectiveness and lead times of alternative recruiting resources in generating enlistment contracts and accessions. The Recruiting Resource Model (RRM) developed in this report considers the relationship among the monthly level and mix of recruiting resources, recruit eligibility policies, accumulated contracts, and training seat targets. It models how these factors combine to produce monthly accessions and the number of enlistment contracts at the fiscal year's end that are scheduled to access in the following fiscal year.

The RRM reflects the complex sequence of events leading to an accession. It consists of a contract production submodel, a Delayed Entry Program (DEP) retention submodel, and a cost allocation submodel. The contract production submodel weighs the trade-offs between economic conditions and resources used to produce overall and high-quality (HQ) enlistment contracts (where HQ reflects the Department of Defense [DoD] standard of contracts where the enlistee has a formal high school diploma and scores in the upper fiftieth percentile of the Armed Forces Qualification Test). Based on the contract characteristics (e.g., HQ contract, quick-ship bonus) and training seat vacancies, contracts are scheduled to leave for basic training (i.e., access into the Army) at a specific time. The time between contract and accession is known as the time in the DEP. The DEP retention submodel captures the probabilistic cancellation of the enlistment contract over these months. The third submodel accounts for the resourcing costs that were paid to achieve the fiscal year's enlistment contracts and accessions.

The contract production model is designed to reflect the Army's business model—namely, team recruiting and the dual missioning of recruiters to recruit for both the Regular (active) Army and the U.S. Army Reserve—of the Army's recruiting enterprise that has been in place since FY 2012. The parameters of the contract production model are estimated using Army and economic data that are signals of the recruiting environment, the Army's spending on measurable recruiting resources, and U.S. Army Recruiting Command (USAREC) missioning at the recruiting company-month level. The contract production model is specified to allow for diminishing returns in resources, including the possibility of threshold and saturation effects for advertising, and for alternative methods of enlistment incentive use (e.g., critical skills or quick-ship bonuses). Whether resourcing, missioning, population, or time-invariant properties of recruiting companies are associated with greater contract production depends on the model's parameters, which are determined by its estimation using the detailed Army data. The estimated model reveals that enlistment contract production is sensitive to all recruiting resources, including recruiters, bonuses, and TV prospect advertising.

Scheduled DEP lengths increase during good recruiting environments, as limited short-term training seat availability necessitates longer wait times. However, DEP attrition rates are greater for contracts with longer wait times, as the enlistees find alternative opportunities. The DEP retention submodel is calibrated based on observed transition rates of contracts being canceled while waiting to access. The transition rates differ by contract quality, type, and scheduled time in the DEP. The cost allocation model accounts for costs based on the contracts that access. Some costs are paid regardless, such as advertising and recruiter costs. However, other costs, such as enlistment incentives, are based on the contract accessing. The cost allocation model accounts for the costs in the month the Army becomes obligated to pay them—that is, the month the recruit signs the enlistment contract (contingent on accession for incentives). Accounting for costs when they are used for contract production links resourcing and cost in a structured way, which permits the creation of an optimization algorithm to identify cost-minimizing resource portfolios.

An optimization algorithm is developed to find the cost-minimizing portfolio of recruiting resources conditional on the recruiting environment and Army-established recruit eligibility policies. The optimization algorithm has three objectives: (1) produce enough accessions to fill each month's training seats; (2) achieve a target number of contracts in the DEP that are scheduled to access in the next fiscal year, also known as the entry pool; and (3) minimize total costs. We refer to the combination of the RRM and the optimization algorithm as the RRM tool. We discuss using the RRM tool to predict execution year accessions and the entry pool for the following year from a specified resourcing plan (i.e., a nonoptimized outcome). We also provide six examples of how the RRM tool can be used to inform policymakers concerning potential resource and policy trade-offs or preparing for alternative recruiting conditions or requirements. These examples include cost trade-offs based on

1. alternative recruiting environments
2. alternative resourcing strategies
3. alternative recruit eligibility policies
4. within-year goal or policy changes
5. five-year planning
6. alternative accession goals.

These examples demonstrate the versatility of the RRM tool for considering trade-offs across the recruiting enterprise. In doing so, it can provide resourcing alternatives that achieve accession goals and potentially save hundreds of millions of resourcing dollars.

The examples demonstrate important strategic-level trade-offs. As the difficulty level of recruiting changes in response to changes in accession requirements or recruiting conditions, success and efficiency require different mixes and levels of recruiting resources and enlistment eligibility policies. In combination with recruiting environment predictions from the Recruiting Difficulty Index tool of Wenger et al. (forthcoming), Army planners can use the RRM tool to consider the potential cost and resourcing requirements for a range of recruiting contingencies. Our example of alternative resource strategies demonstrates that a strategy emphasizing one resource in lieu of other resources (e.g., bonuses when policymakers are reactive to a difficult recruiting environment rather than being proactive in planning for it) can be substantially more expensive than using a mix of resources. Additionally, we show that changing recruit eligibility policies can reduce recruiting resource costs substantially. When the RRM tool is used in combination with the Recruit Selection Tool (Orvis et al., forthcoming), policymakers can consider the first-term costs associated with broadening eligibility criteria in addition to the recruiting costs. Within-year analyses demonstrate the substantial cost savings and higher probability of goal achievement when resources are adjusted optimally to deal with changing accession requirements. The five-year planning example demonstrates how policymakers can use the RRM tool to determine efficient and effective resourcing and eligibility policies to meet long-range recruiting objectives and to weigh the desirability and feasibility of alternative objectives in supporting end-strength goals.

The RRM tool is not prescriptive. It informs Army planners and leaders regarding potential trade-offs in monthly recruiting resources conditional on recruit eligibility policies and the recruiting environment, over both short and long time periods. It does this through a coherent, mathematically based model that yields consistent results with explicit assumptions and caveats. Consequently, it represents a step forward in helping Army leaders shape a cost-efficient strategy capable of achieving Army's accession requirements. The continued success of the RRM tool will require updating the model to reflect the current effectiveness of recruiting resources, and future enhancements could include integration with existing planning and budgeting models to make the RRM tool a budgeting resource in addition to a strategic resource.

Acknowledgments

We are appreciative of the support of our sponsor, Mr. Mark Davis, the Deputy Assistant Secretary of the Army for Marketing, and his office for their support of the research documented in this report, including John Jessup, Shawn McCurry, Alicia McCleary, Jeff Sterling, John Keeter, Jan Jedrych, James Ortiz, LTC Chike Robertson, MAJ Trent Geisler, Heather Whitehouse, and Terrance Mann. At Headquarters, Department of the Army, G-1, we are grateful for feedback at different phases of this project from COL Joanne Moore, Mr. Roy Wallace, MAJ Larry Tobin, LTC Tom Kucik, CPT Eric O'Connor, Dr. Bob Steinrauf, and LTC Robert Nowicki. We also wish to express our thanks to COL Ken Burkman, Mike Nelson, Joe Baird, and Rick Ayer at the U.S. Army Recruiting Command. At RAND, we would like to thank Christine DeMartini, Jan Hanley, Laurie McDonald, Teague Ruder, and Whitney Dudley for their programming assistance, and Chris Guo and Steven Garber for their technical expertise in the initial stages of this research. Finally, we received helpful comments from our reviewers, Jim Hosek of RAND and Matt Goldberg of IDA.

Abbreviations

AFQT	Armed Forces Qualification Test
AMRG	Army Marketing and Research Group
BLS	Bureau of Labor Statistics
CPI-U	Consumer Price Index–Urban Consumers
DEP	Delayed Entry Program
DMDC	Defense Manpower Data Center
DoD	Department of Defense
EIRB	Enlistment Incentive Review Board
FY	fiscal year
GA	graduate alpha
HQ	high quality
HQDA	Headquarters, Department of the Army
HRC	Human Resources Command
IET	Initial Entry Training
MOS	Military Occupational Specialty
NPS	non–prior service
ODCS	Office of the Deputy Chief of Staff
RA	Regular Army
RCM	recruiting contract month
RRM	Recruiting Resource Model
RSM	recruiting ship month
TA	Total Army
USAR	U.S. Army Reserve
USAREC	U.S. Army Recruiting Command

CHAPTER ONE

Introduction

Background

Since 2001, between 57,000 and 80,000 enlisted soldiers per fiscal year have accessed into the Regular Army (RA). To accomplish this accession level, the U.S. Army Recruiting Command (USAREC) must sign 8–10 percent more enlistment contracts to account for individuals not following through with their contracts.

As a result, the Army's recruiting enterprise is substantial, with over 8,000 recruiters placed at over 1,300 recruiting centers across the country (as of May 2017), a national advertising campaign directed by the Army Marketing and Research Group (AMRG), and an enlistment incentive (i.e., bonus) structure managed at least quarterly by the Enlistment Incentive Review Board (EIRB). In fiscal year (FY) 2008 and FY 2009, nearly $2.0 billion in 2016 dollars was spent per year on recruiting.[1] The average

---

[1] This estimate is provided to give the reader a sense of magnitude and is based only on marketing and incentive costs and required recruiter numbers provided by the Office of the Deputy Chief of Staff, G-1 (ODCS G-1): marketing, $328 million; enlistment incentives, $669 million; and recruiters, $944 million. Both marketing and enlistment incentives are inflated by the Bureau of Labor Statistics (BLS) Consumer Price Index–Urban Consumers (CPI-U) to 2016 dollars, while the figure for recruiters reflects the average cost per recruiter in 2016 ($118,000 per recruiter) provided by Headquarters, Department of the Army (HQDA). The actual number of recruiters in the field likely deviates from the required recruiting force due to USAREC's operational requirements. Enlistment incentives reflect current and anniversary payments, not the amounts obligated to contracts written during the fiscal year. Recruiters, advertising, and enlistment bonuses offered to prospective recruits peaked in FY 2007–2008. Because bonuses are paid upon completion of Initial Entry Training (IET)—and for bonuses over $10,000, the remainder is paid out over the remainder of the recruit's term of enlistment— the actual costs incurred by the Army peaked in FY 2008–2009.

over FY 2001 to FY 2014 was $1.5 billion in 2016 dollars. The average annual cost of an accession accounting only for recruiters, bonuses, and marketing ranged from $15,500 (FY 2004) to $27,700 (FY 2009), with the average cost over FY 2001 to FY 2014 being $20,300.[2] The variation in cost reflects differences in both recruiting environments and the accession mission. When difficult environments and large missions combine, as in FY 2005–2008, the marginal cost of a recruiting contract can be far larger than the average contract cost.

Recruiting resources differ not only in their cost per additional contract produced but also in time elapsed between resource use and productive response. For example, bonuses have the most immediate impact, but are relatively expensive. Additional recruiters and advertising are less costly, but require more planning time and time to produce enlistment contracts. Training seats are distributed unevenly across the fiscal year, adding another component to the Army planners' calculus. Resourcing needs to be planned such that contracts are produced with sufficient lead time to ensure that the enlistees fill the available training seats.

Resources are not the only policy levers that the Army employs to achieve its recruiting mission. The Army uses a suite of recruiting resources and recruit eligibility policies to achieve its annual accession requirement. Department of Defense (DoD) Instruction 1145.01 establishes benchmarks for recruiting success, including 60 percent of fiscal year accessions scoring in the upper fiftieth percentile of the Armed Forces Qualification Test (AFQT) national distribution, and 90 percent high school diploma graduates. Consistent with DoD practice, this report will refer to enlistments that exhibit both of these characteristics as high-quality (HQ) enlistments. DoD Instruction 1304.26 established additional qualifications for enlistments related to age, citizenship, education, aptitude, medical condition, physical fitness, dependency, conduct, and drug and alcohol use. Importantly, this instruction also establishes criteria for providing waivers based on current or past medical, dependent, conduct, and drug issues. The issuance of waivers is

---

[2]   We follow the same methodology as in footnote 1 and take the average over this time period, not accounting for differences in annual accession requirements.

devolved to the services. Finally, while annual Army enlistment targets typically focus on non–prior service (NPS) recruits, HQDA regularly establishes Prior Service Business Rules that guide the ability of recruiters to enlist individuals with prior military experience. Determination of a potential prior service recruit's eligibility to reenter the Army is typically based on his or her previous service record, Military Occupational Specialty (MOS), and last pay grade, or the recruit's willingness to be retrained in a limited set of high-need occupations.

As with recruiting resources, recruit eligibility policies are expanded during difficult recruiting conditions and limited at other times. For example, analysis of contracting data indicates that prior service accessions from FY 2001 to FY 2014 ranged from a low of 921 in FY 2012 to over 13,000 in FY 2007. Additionally, accessions fell below established education and aptitude benchmarks during FY 2006–2008,[3] and waivers exceeded 20 percent in FY 2007. Expanding recruit eligibility can offer a less expensive means of achieving recruiting goals. Waiver rates and quality benchmarks represent barriers to entry that, if relaxed, could permit an expansion of the potential recruit pool.

In ever-changing recruiting environments, the relative value of alternative resource and eligibility policy approaches to meeting the accession requirements will vary. There is a strong association between the tightening of the external labor market (i.e., the civilian unemployment rate decreases) and the ability of USAREC to meet its monthly contract mission. Wenger et al. (forthcoming) examines the relationship between the fraction of contract mission achieved for graduate alphas (GAs) and the unemployment rate. GAs are HQ contracts that are available to ship at any time because they have already graduated from high school. However, they are also in demand in the civilian labor market. A simple regression relating a monthly measure of the fraction of contract mission achieved for GAs to the civilian unemployment rate has an R-squared of 0.59, which indicates that 59 percent of the vari-

---

[3]   During this period, the Office of the Secretary of Defense gave the Army permission to enlist up to 10 percent of its recruits into the Tier Two Attrition Screen program. In effect, this increased the OSD-approved ceiling for youth with Tier Two education credentials from 10 percent of accessions to 20 percent.

ance in the fraction of contract mission achieved for GAs is explained by variance in the unemployment rate.

Purpose of the Report

Understanding how recruiting resources and recruit eligibility policies work together as a system under varying recruiting requirements and environments is critical for decisionmakers who want to use their limited resources to efficiently and effectively achieve the Army's accession requirements. This research builds on earlier work by manpower researchers, including many from RAND Arroyo Center, on the effectiveness and lead times of alternative recruiting resources in generating enlistment contracts and accessions. The Recruiting Resource Model (RRM) developed in this report considers the relationship among the monthly level and mix of recruiting resources, recruit eligibility policies, accumulated contracts, and training seat targets. It models how these factors combine to produce monthly accessions and the number of enlistment contracts at the fiscal year's end that are scheduled to access in the following fiscal year.

Our Approach

The RRM reflects the complex sequence of events leading to an accession. It consists of a contract production submodel, a Delayed Entry Program (DEP) retention submodel, and a cost allocation submodel. The contract production submodel weighs the trade-offs between economic conditions and resources used to produce overall and HQ enlistment contracts. Based on the contract characteristics (e.g., HQ contract, quick-ship bonus) and training seat vacancies, contracts are scheduled to leave for basic training (i.e., access into the Army) at a specific time. The time between contract and accession is known as the time in the DEP. The DEP retention submodel captures the probabilistic attrition of the contract from the DEP (and out of the potential accession pool) over these months. The third submodel accounts for the resourcing costs that were paid to achieve the fiscal year's enlistment contracts and accessions.

The contract production model is designed to reflect the business model of the Army's recruiting enterprise in place between FY 2012 and FY 2015. The parameters of the contract production model are estimated using Army and economic data that are signals of the recruiting environment, the Army's spending on measurable recruiting resources, and USAREC missioning by the recruiting company-month level. The contract production model is specified to allow for diminishing returns in resources, including the possibility of threshold and saturation effects for advertising, and for alternative methods of enlistment incentive use (e.g., MOS or quick-ship). The contract production model is designed around recruiters—if there is no recruiter at a recruiting company or that company has no contract mission or there are no youth living in the recruiting company's geographic bounds, then the contract production model would yield no contracts. Recruiting resources and environment may augment the recruiters' productive ability, and a greater mission—all else equal—may incentivize contract production. Additionally, recruiting companies with more youth in their geographic bounds may produce more contracts, and there may be persistent differences between regions based on unobserved factors such as differential propensity to enlist. Whether resourcing, missioning, population, or time-invariant properties of recruiting companies are associated with greater contract production depends on the model's parameters, which are determined by its estimation using the detailed Army data.

Scheduled DEP lengths increase during good recruiting environments, as limited short-term training seat availability necessitates longer wait times. However, DEP attrition rates are greater for contracts with longer wait times, as the enlistees find alternative opportunities. The DEP retention submodel is calibrated based on observed transition rates of contracts being canceled while waiting to access. The transition rates differ by contract quality, type, and scheduled time in the DEP. The cost allocation model accounts for costs based on the contracts that access. Some costs are paid regardless, such as advertising and recruiter costs. However, other costs, such as enlistment incentives, are based on the contract accessing. The cost allocation model accounts for the costs in the month the Army becomes obligated to pay them—the month the enlistee signs the contract, or the month a TV commercial is aired. Accounting for costs when they are used for contract production links resourcing and cost in a structured way, which permits the creation of an optimization algorithm to identify cost-minimizing resource portfolios.

We develop an optimization algorithm designed to find the cost-minimizing portfolio of recruiting resources conditional on the recruiting environment and Army-established recruit eligibility policies. The optimization algorithm has three objectives: (1) produce enough accessions to fill each month's training seats; (2) achieve a target number of contracts in the DEP that are scheduled to access in the next fiscal year, also known as the entry pool; and (3) minimize total costs. We refer to the combination of the RRM and the optimization algorithm as the RRM tool. We provide a number of examples for how the RRM tool may be used, including predicting execution year accessions and the entry pool for the following year from a specified resourcing plan (i.e., a nonoptimized outcome), and six optimized outcomes:

1. Determine a cost-minimizing resourcing plan for a fiscal year (i.e., optimized outcome)
2. Compare the sensitivity of resourcing plans under alternative recruiting environments
3. Compare alternative resourcing plans (e.g., incentive-centric versus an optimized resource strategy)
4. Compare cost trade-offs of alternative eligibility policies
5. Consider within-year changes in resourcing plans necessary to achieve an accession mission (e.g., halfway through the fiscal year, what policy levers can be used to achieve the accession mission and what would be the cost-minimizing portfolio for the remaining six months of the fiscal year)
6. Consider multiple year resourcing scenarios.

The RRM is a versatile framework that can be adapted and updated to reflect changes in the efficacy of resources, changes in the structure of the recruiting enterprise, and lessons learned about the responsiveness of contract production to changes in recruit eligibility policies. The RRM tool reported on and developed in this report should be viewed as a resource that can help Army leaders understand the complex trade-offs involved in recruiting, and that can be updated and improved to meet the Army's operational needs.

Organization of the Report

Chapter Two describes the use of recruiting resources, enlistment eligibility policies, and the recruiting environment since FY 2003, and discusses past research on enlistment supply. Chapter Three discusses the data we use in this analysis, as well as past measures of enlistment supply's responsiveness to recruiting resources and the recruiting environment. Chapter Four presents an overview of the model and discusses each submodel in depth. It concludes with an in-sample validation test. Chapter Five discusses how the optimization algorithm works, and provides six examples of analyses using the RRM tool that can clarify the trade-offs in alternative resourcing policies, trade-offs for expanding recruit eligibility, and extensions for long-term budgeting or efficient short-term reallocation of resources for achieving a change in annual accession goals. Chapter Six provides our conclusions and recommendations.

CHAPTER TWO

Overview of Recent Resource Use and Eligibility Policies

This chapter describes accession goals and key measures of the recruiting environment since FY 2003, and then describes how recruiting resources were used and recruit eligibility policies were set to achieve those goals.[1] We do not detail every policy lever used during this time frame, but instead focus on some of the most consistently used resource and policy levers. We conclude by briefly reviewing past work on enlistment supply and where this model fits within the context of past work.

Recruiting Goals and Environment

From 2003 to 2015, accession goals varied from a high of 80,000 to a low of 57,000 enlisted accessions. During this time frame, the accession goal was missed only once, in 2005. From FY 2005 to FY 2008, the Army set high enlistment goals to increase RA end strength to 540,000. These numbers, while high compared with recent accession goals, are low compared with history. As detailed in Table 2.1, during FY 1980– 1984 the average recruiting goal was 144,000. The Army has failed to achieve its accession goals three times since 1980: FY 1998, FY 1999, and FY 2005 (Accession Policy, 2017). These times have been characterized by declining unemployment, an initially high fraction of AFQT I-IIIA recruits in the year (or initial year) of the failure, and lower

---

[1] FY 2003 represents the first complete fiscal year where we have consistently collected Army data for recruiters, missioning, and contract level.

quality achievement in the year(s) immediately following the missed recruiting goals. This is suggestive evidence that policy response to a worsening recruiting environment, at least in terms of relaxing eligibility restrictions, occurred too late.

Wenger et al. (forthcoming) evaluated a number of alternative measures of the recruiting environment. The most indicative of their measures of the recruiting environment was the fraction of contract mission achieved for GAs, defined as a high school graduate in the top fiftieth percentile of the AFQT. GAs are the most likely recruits to be supply constrained, and since they have already graduated, they can access at any time. Figure 2.1 demonstrates the monthly relationship between the contract mission achievement rate and the civilian unemployment rate. Unemployment and contract mission achievement are strongly related. After missing contract mission in FY 2005, the Army responded by expanding eligibility and increasing recruiting resources, as we will demonstrate next. The response to expanded eligibility can be seen in Figure 2.1 by contrasting all RA contract mission achievement with GA contract mission achievement. During FY 2006–2008, the Army leaned heavily on expanded eligibility to meet recruiting objectives, driving RA contract mission achievement closer to 100 percent, while GA contract mission achievement remained persistently low. The relaxation of eligibility criteria is primarily reflected in Table 2.1 through a decrease in Tier 1 enlistments.

Recruiting Resources

This report focuses on three recruiting resources: recruiters, enlistment incentives, and advertising. Recruiters are assigned to centers, which report to recruiting companies. Figure 2.2 depicts changes in USAREC companies and centers from FY 2003 to FY 2015. After accession mission failure in FY 2005, many additional recruiters were added to the recruiting field. The number of recruiters remained relatively flat through FY 2007, at which point more recruiters were placed at centers. The number of RA recruiters at centers in the 50 states and Washington, D.C., reached its peak in June 2009. As recruiting conditions improved,

Table 2.1
End Strength, Recruiting Goals and Achievement, and Recruit Quality
(FY 1980–2015)

Fiscal Year	Overall End Strength	Enlisted End Strength	Recruiting Goals	Recruiting Actual	Tier 1 — High School Degree	Top 50th Percentile AFQT	Percentage of HQ	Adult Civilian Unemp. Rate
1980[a]	777,036	673,944	172,800	173,228	54.0	22.0	21.0	6.8
1981[a]	781,419	675,087	136,800	137,916	80.0	34.0	29.0	7.4
1982	780,391	672,699	125,100	130,198	86.0	46.0	39.0	9.1
1983	779,643	669,364	144,500	145,287	88.0	53.0	45.0	10.1
1984	780,180	667,711	141,757	142,266	91.0	54.0	47.0	7.8
1985	780,787	666,557	125,300	125,443	91.0	61.0	52.0	7.3
1986	780,980	666,668	135,250	135,530	91.0	63.0	54.0	7.1
1987	780,815	668,410	132,000	133,016	91.0	67.0	58.0	6.4
1988	771,847	660,445	115,000	115,386	83.1	65.0	52.0	5.6
1989	769,741	658,321	119,875	120,535	89.9	62.2	55.0	5.3
1990	750,589	641,341	87,000	89,620	95.0	67.0	62.0	5.4
1991	725,445	682,004	78,241	78,241	97.6	82.4	69.4	6.6
1992	611,305	511,834	75,000	77,583	98.7	77.4	76.4	7.4
1993	572,423	480,379	76,900	77,563	93.0	69.7	64.6	7.1
1994	541,343	452,513	68,000	68,039	92.9	70.2	64.1	6.4
1995	508,559	422,073	62,929	62,929	93.8	69.0	63.6	5.6
1996	491,103	406,502	73,400	73,418	93.4	66.7	60.9	5.5
1997	491,707	408,337	82,000	82,088	90.0	67.5	57.8	5.1
1998	483,880	401,188	72,550	71,733	89.8	67.3	56.6	4.6
1999	479,426	398,138	74,500	68,209	88.2	61.5	52.2	4.3
2000	482,170	401,414	80,000	80,113	86.5	65.3	53.6	4.0
2001	480,801	400,461	75,800	75,855	83.4	64.4	52.5	4.3
2002	486,543	404,305	79,500	79,585	84.4	69.9	57.3	5.7

Table 2.1—Continued

Fiscal Year	Overall End Strength	Enlisted End Strength	Recruiting Goals	Recruiting Actual	Tier 1 — High School Degree	Top 50th Percentile AFQT	Percentage of HQ	Adult Civilian Unemp. Rate
2003	499,301	414,769	73,800	74,132	85.8	72.4	60.0	6.0
2004	499,543	412,324	77,000	77,586	85.9	71.5	60.9	5.6
2005	492,728	406,923	80,000	73,373	81.8	67.1	56.2	5.2
2006	505,402	419,353	80,000	80,635	73.3	60.1	45.2	4.7
2007	522,017	433,109	80,000	80,407	70.1	60.9	44.2	4.5
2008	543,645	451,846	80,000	80,517	73.7	62.0	45.6	5.3
2009	553,044	457,980	65,000	70,045	85.5	66.4	54.1	8.5
2010	566,045	467,248	74,500	74,577	96.9	63.9	61.4	9.7
2011	565,463	463,605	64,000	64,019	97.3	62.7	60.6	9.2
2012	550,064	447,075	58,000	60,490	95.4	64.2	60.0	8.3
2013	532,426	428,923	69,000	69,154	98.4	62.0	60.5	7.6
2014	508,210	406,519	57,000	57,101	94.1	61.4	57.6	6.5
2015	491,365	392,327	59,000	59,117	97.9	60.0	57.9	5.4
2016[b]	475,400	378,778	62,500	62,682	94.7	60.3	55.8	4.9

NOTE: End-strength data collected from Department of Army's Annual Budget Report to the President, with the exception of 1980–1983 data, which were collected from historical reports provided to the Defense Manpower Data Center (DMDC) in 1996 from the Washington Headquarters Services, Statistical Information Analysis Division; accession goals, achievement, and quality measures collected from Accession Policy (2017); and the unemployment rate is collected from the Bureau of Labor Statistics (BLS).[a] 1980–1981 Armed Services Vocational Aptitude Battery (ASVAB) misnorming, DMDC Historical Data.[b] Data are preliminary and have not been validated by the Army.

fewer recruiters were needed to achieve accession goals. Starting in the last quarter of FY 2011, USAREC consolidated its operations, reducing the number of centers and recruiters. The consolidation was primarily done within recruiting companies.[2]

---

[2]   The geographic boundaries of recruiting companies and centers do change from time to time, and this was more prevalent during the FY 2012 time period.

Figure 2.1
Contract Mission Achievement for GAs and the Civilian Unemployment Rate (FY 2003–2015)

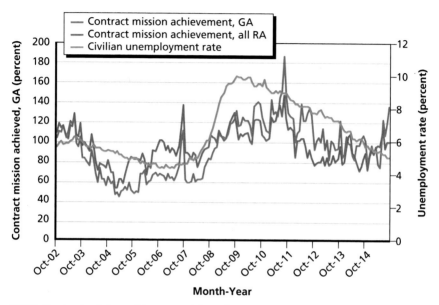

NOTE: Contract mission achievement is based on USAREC and Human Resources Command (HRC) administrative data discussed in Chapter Three. BLS produces the monthly adult civilian unemployment rate.

RAND RR2364A-2.1

The use of enlistment incentives has also changed dramatically over time, as demonstrated in Figures 2.3 and 2.4. From June 2003 to June 2005, the Army sharply expanded GA MOS bonus eligibility for contracts written from 55 percent to 90 percent and quick-ship bonuses from 4 percent in March 2003 to 58 percent in March 2005. As recruiting conditions remained tough, both bonus levels and eligibility expanded. At their height in September 2007, 89 percent of GA enlistment contracts received a quick-ship bonus, with the average bonus being $25,000 (equivalent to about $29,300 in May 2017). During FY 2009, quick-ship bonuses were abruptly turned off, and MOS bonuses were reduced significantly in both level and eligibility. During FY 2013–2014, GA eligibility for MOS bonuses was restricted; however, bonus levels were increased. Starting in FY 2015, the Army

Figure 2.2
Recruiters and Recruiting Companies and Centers (FY 2003–2015)

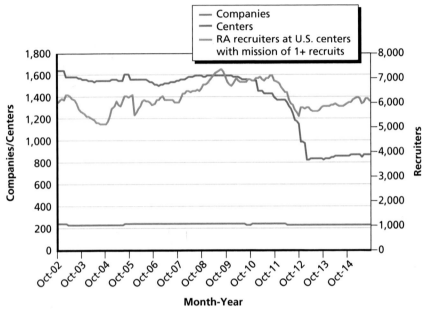

NOTE: This information is derived from administrative data provided by USAREC
described in Chapter Three. Companies and centers reflect locations within the 50
states and the District of Columbia where at least one recruiter is assigned and the
location is assigned a production mission of one or more recruits; RA recruiters
reflects recruiters assigned to such locations.
RAND RR2364A-2.2

expanded its use of quick-ship and MOS bonuses. During the first five
months of FY 2017, GA eligibility for bonuses was around 47 percent
for MOS bonuses and 30 percent for quick-ship bonuses, and average
bonus levels were approximately $12,000 and $15,000, respectively.[3]

The monthly data for recruiters and enlistment incentives reflect
granular data at the contract level for enlistment incentives and recruiter
level for recruiters and centers. There is not currently an analogue that
has been consistently collected over time for advertising. The closest

---

[3]   Based on reported information provided by ODCS G-1 in March 2017.

Figure 2.3
GA MOS Bonus Levels and Eligibility (FY 2003–2015)

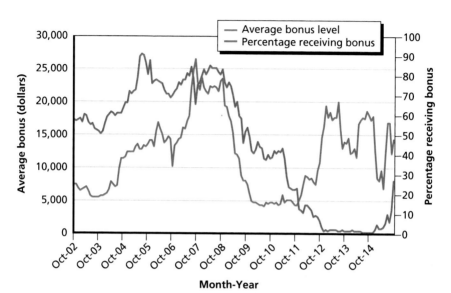

NOTE: This information is derived from administrative data described in Chapter Three. We define MOS bonuses as bonuses that target a specific MOS (i.e., critical skills). Average bonus levels reflect the average bonus of contracts signed in a recruiting contract month conditional on receipt of an MOS bonus. These values are reported in current-year dollars. The fraction receiving the bonus is calculated based on all contracts signed in a recruiting contract month. The realized bonus level may reflect additional bonus categories that an enlistee also qualifies for.
RAND RR2364A-2.3

consistently collected data for advertising come from DD804-4, which is a required report to Congress that splits out a service's spending by a number of measures, including TV advertising. However, these data are reported only at the national level, are not broken out into monthly figures, and conflate advertising across submarkets (e.g., Army medical advertising). The numbers are still telling regarding the positive correlation between advertising and recruiting, as noted in Table 2.2. From FY 2003 to FY 2008, advertising increased from $250 million to $423 million. As recruiting conditions improved, the advertising budget decreased sharply, to $190 million in FY 2011, before increasing to $311 million by FY 2015.

Figure 2.4
GA Quick-Ship Bonus Levels and Take Rates (FY 2003–2015)

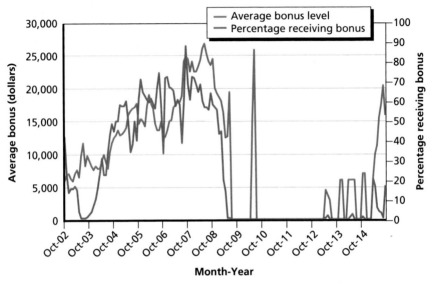

NOTE: This information is derived from administrative data described in Chapter Three. We define quick-ship bonuses as bonuses that require a very short DEP period in order to qualify. Average bonus levels reflect the average bonus of contracts signed in a recruiting contract month conditional on receipt of a quick-ship bonus. These values are reported in current-year dollars. The fraction receiving the bonus is calculated based on all contracts signed in a recruiting contract month. The realized bonus level may reflect additional bonus categories that an enlistee also qualifies for. The odd high average bonus level during FY 2010 reflects a very targeted bonus given to very few contracts.
RAND RR2364A-2.4

Recruit Eligibility Policies

As mentioned in the introduction, one of the Army's main recruiting objectives is to achieve HQ accessions. HQ enlistees qualify for a wider breadth of MOS, have fewer conduct issues, and are much less likely to attrit. However, during difficult recruiting conditions, eligibility policies have become a lever that can be used to meet the primary recruiting objective: the accession goal.

A key policy is the number of enlistment waivers the Army chooses to grant. Waivers can be given for a number of reasons, but the two

Table 2.2
Fiscal Year Advertising Expenditures

Fiscal Year	Advertising ($M)
2001	176
2002	210
2003	250
2004	264
2005	307
2006	345
2007	388
2008	423
2009	293
2010	200
2011	190
2012	198
2013	192
2014	225
2015	311

NOTE: Total advertising in millions of current dollars. The data
were collected from DD804-4 reports to Congress and reflect
all advertising costs, including television, radio, direct mail,
promotional items, market research, print materials, internet
activity, events, and other related advertising costs such as
the cost of the advertising agency's labor. These expenditure
reports are available only at the annual and national levels.

most common waivers used during difficult recruiting conditions are
medical and nondrug, misdemeanor conduct waivers. We present in
Figure 2.5 monthly variation in waivers by contract month and year.
Conduct waivers were heavily expanded after FY 2005 and remained
high until partway through FY 2009, at which point they were dramatically reduced. Medical waivers, on the other hand, have shown less

Figure 2.5
NPS Medical and Conduct Waivers (FY 2003–2014)

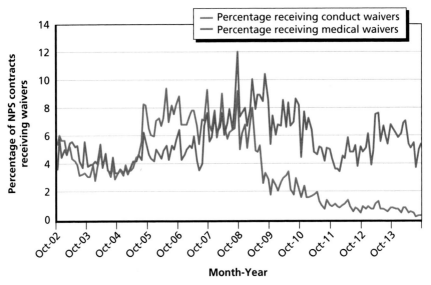

NOTE: This information is derived from administrative data described in Chapter Three. Month-year refers to the month the contract is signed. However, waiver calculations are based on accessions, not contracts. Waivers include both DEP and accession waivers. The figure stops at the end of FY 2014 because we cannot see all of the contracts signed in FY 2015 that accessed (since our data end in FY 2015). We need to be able to observe accessions to determine whether waivers are given.
RAND RR2364A-2.5

association with the recruiting environment, but their use has changed notably over time, from less than 4 percent at the start of FY 2005 to as high as 12 percent at the end of FY 2008.

Likewise, quality targets and limits on enlistments among persons with prior military service have been relaxed during difficult recruiting conditions. We present month-year variation in quality and prior service enlistments in Figure 2.6. In FY 2005, quality goals were notably reduced, likely reflecting an effort to meet accession goals. Quality marks remained low from FY 2006 to FY 2008, in some months dropping below 40 percent HQ, before rising during FY 2009 as the recruiting market improved and tougher quality constraints were imposed.

Figure 2.6
HQ and Prior Service Contracts (FY 2003–2014)

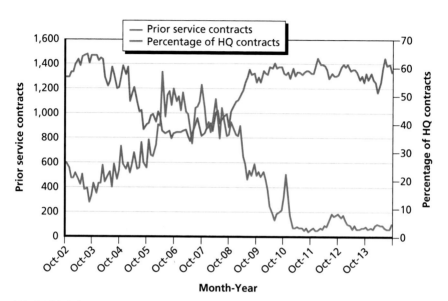

NOTE: This information is derived from administrative data described in Chapter Three.
RAND RR2364A-2.6

Prior service is an important eligibility characteristic that can be expanded during difficult recruiting conditions. During FY 2006–2008, in the majority of months, more than 1,000 prior service contracts were signed, leading to thousands of prior service accessions by month. From FY 2012 to FY 2014, the ODCS G-1 mission letter routinely targeted zero prior service accessions—a sharp change from half a decade earlier. However, even during this more recent period, the zero prior service targets were not achieved.

Related Research

There is an extensive line of research that has focused on enlistment supply—that is, the willingness of individuals to enlist in the military. This research has evaluated the responsiveness of enlistments to resource use, including education incentives, enlistment bonuses, advertising, and recruiters. Rarely has it touched on eligibility policy, as it has remained focused on the most supply-constrained portion of the potential enlistment population: HQ contracts. This literature consists mostly of models estimated on data prior to FY 2012. Asch, Hosek, and Warner (2007) provide a review of post-drawdown estimates from this literature, covering primarily the 1990s. An important caveat of this literature is that few estimates result from causal analyses, meaning that the estimated economic models measure the association between the use of a resource and contract production rather than measure how much greater contract production is because of the use of a resource. Measuring associations has led to biased estimates for some recruiting resources. The standard example is enlistment bonuses. A simple correlation between enlistment bonuses and contracts might yield a negative association, reflecting the use of bonuses when recruiting conditions are difficult. Even controlling for other factors in a regression context may be insufficient, particularly if only national measures are available. Recent research—including that of Warner, Simon, and Payne (2001, 2003) and Asch et al. (2010)—has circumvented the endogeneity problem by relying on geographical variation (in these cases, at the state level) in the response to enlistment incentives to identify the relationship between contract production and enlistment incentives. An older study by Polich, Dertouzos, and Press (1986) evaluated a bonus experiment in which a subset of recruiting regions were offered a more generous enlistment incentive. This type of experiment more closely approximates a causal measure because it compares the enlistment responses of regions that differ only in the level of bonuses offered and terms of service the bonuses are linked to.[4] In general, whether through an experimental or a nonexperimental technique exploiting

---

[4]   Similar national experiments were carried out to assess alternative educational incentives (the Educational Assistance Test Program); combined active and reserve service (the 2+2+4 Recruiting Experiment); expansion of the market to youth without traditional high school diplomas (GED Plus) and to youth wanting to attend college for up to two years after enlisting but before accessing (College First); and the expansion effects of a home ownership/business start-up incentive (Army Advantage Fund).

geographical variation, this literature has found that HQ contract production is responsive to enlistment bonuses, and the measured response using these techniques has been similar. Bonuses tend to be a relatively expensive resource when compared with recruiters, but less expensive than raising basic pay. This literature has not distinguished between enlistment bonuses for shipping quickly and enlistment incentives for critical skills.

Whereas the role of recruiters and enlistment incentives are frequently accounted for in these models, detailed data on advertising are less common. Three studies make use of detailed advertising data below the national level (Dertouzos and Garber, 2003; Dertouzos, 2009; Warner, Simon, and Payne, 2001), and all three find that advertising is strongly associated with HQ enlistment contracts. Warner, Simon, and Payne (2001) evaluate all three resources in the same modeling framework; they find that the cost of producing an additional contract from advertising for the Army was less expensive than using recruiters or enlistment incentives. Efficiency suggests that the lowest-cost mixture of resources should be used to produce the last contract. Given Warner, Simon, and Payne's (2001) estimates, recruiting objectives could have been achieved at a lower cost by increasing advertising or recruiters while decreasing the use of enlistment incentives.

The challenge with the aforementioned analysis is that these estimates represent a point in time. There is no guarantee that resources will be equally productive as time progresses, or that recruiting practices will remain the same, or that the propensity to serve will remain the same. Consequently, it is important to update models of enlistment supply to ensure they reflect current circumstances. For example, with the introduction of the 9-11 GI bill in 2009, the role of college funds as an enlistment incentive has been effectively eliminated. Additionally, the role of recruiter effort in the Army has changed as USAREC moved away from individual missioning toward team recruiting, where missions are handled at the center and company levels. Such changes can affect the estimated productivity of enlistment bonuses (which were typically offered alongside education incentives in the 1990s) or recruiter write rates (which have decreased since 2001).

Additionally, the previous analyses were not designed to allow for Army planners to consider alternative combinations of resourcing policies. In part this is because the models would need to capture other parts of the recruiting process, like recruit eligibility policies, non-HQ production, and DEP attrition and accession. Additionally, allowing Army planners to try alternative policies would require a tool they could use for balancing resources and an optimization algorithm for weighing one resource relative to another. Finally, it would require a model that balances all resources; and, as previously mentioned, consistently collecting detailed advertising data has remained elusive, with the last detailed Army advertising data collected from 2002 to 2004 (Dertouzos, 2009). The development of the RRM tool, described in Chapters Four and Five, is meant to address the need for a dynamic and interactive policy tool that will allow Army planners to consider alternative scenarios based on a contract production function that captures trade-offs across the major recruiting resources.[5]

In lieu of experimental data, the RRM tool faces many of the same empirical challenges mentioned above. However, it updates models of contract production to reflect recent recruiting experience, the present use of enlistment incentives, and current recruiting practices. It also provides alternative framing, focusing not on enlistment supply (i.e., the willingness of a qualified individual to enlist) but on the productive potential of a recruiting company over time as resources, eligibility policies, and recruiting conditions change. As part of this research, we went to great lengths to work with the Army's ad agency and AMRG to ensure that the requisite advertising data were collected for television; in future work we aim to analyze the relationship between internet and social media advertising and enlistment. Additionally, the RRM tool was developed in such a way as to allow Army planners to consider a variety of resourcing and eligibility alternatives, while also making the model flexible enough that it can be updated. The aim is to provide a

---

[5] The RRM tool differs from Goldberg, Kimko, and Li (2015), who predict future outcomes using only recruiters and exogenous variables outside the Army's control. Their model may be effective at predicting recruiting environment; however, it cannot be used to consider alternative resourcing policies.

planning tool that can improve resourcing efficiency and allow senior leaders to consider trade-offs between eligibility policy and resources while also improving the likelihood of the Army achieving accession and recruit quality goals.

CHAPTER THREE

Data Used for This Study

Data were collected from a number of sources and broadly divided into three categories: military data, advertising data, and economic and demographic data. In this chapter, we review the data available to inform our study. We conclude this chapter with some more technical notes about the timing of when measures were calculated. The end result of the data collection is a company-level analytical dataset with monthly measures covering August 2002 through September 2015.

We conduct our analysis at the recruiting company-month level because it is the most disaggregated geography for which we have consistent Army measures. A major objective of our data collection was to ensure that observed values correctly correspond to a specific month and recruiting company. For example, we are cautious to ensure resources and outputs are allocated to the correct geography. In this way, we ensure resources, such as recruiters and advertising, can be associated with the contract production in the appropriate area and at the same time.

Army Data

Army data are drawn primarily from databases maintained by the U.S. Army HRC and USAREC, and strategic guidance is issued by ODCS G-1 within HQDA.

Data on recruiters are collected from a recruiter database maintained by USAREC for purposes of tracking each recruiter's current status and assignment. The file reflects a monthly snapshot of each recruiter, an indicator of his or her company and center assignment, and an indicator of whether the recruiter is on production (versus on leave or other alternative duty assignment). It covers the time period from August 2002 until September 2015.

Data on contract missioning are collected through a contract missioning system used and maintained by USAREC to allocate and report contract mission goals and achievements. It records key measures at the recruiting brigade, battalion, company, and center levels. The system is populated by USAREC allocating a monthly mission to each brigade. Each brigade then allocates a contract mission to each of its battalions. Each battalion then allocates a contract mission to each of its companies. Finally, each company then allocates a contract mission to each of its recruiting centers. This system can be used to generate monthly measures of the contract mission at the respective brigade, battalion, company, or center level for key missioning categories including GAs, senior alphas (i.e., a high school senior scoring in the top fiftieth percentile on the AFQT), and others (i.e., not GAs or senior alphas) in both the RA and U.S. Army Reserve (USAR) components. From the missioning and recruiter data, we compute the number of recruiters on production at the center level by summing the number of recruiters at centers with a production mission of at least one recruit, and the monthly GA contract mission by summing the mission assigned to recruiting centers in the 50 states and the District of Columbia with at least one recruiter on production at the center.[1] Requiring a center to have at least one recruiter and a nonzero contract mission is done to control for the opening and closing of centers, which can spuriously increase the estimate of the true mission assigned in a month.

Data on contracts written and which of the recruits accessed are collected from the RA Analyst file maintained by HRC. This file captures every contract written from FY 2001 to the present. It reports key measures of these contracts, including when the contract was signed, the recruiter associated with the contract, the cumulative amount and types of bonuses associated with the contract, educational background and

---

[1]   In some fiscal years, the recording of missioning at the center level is inconsistent. In these cases, we use missioning at the company level.

the outcomes of military qualification tests, the projected accession date for the contract, and the actual accession date for the contract, among other variables. From these data, we compute key monthly contract measures including the average DEP length, monthly attrition rates based on time scheduled in the DEP, the fraction of recruits accepting each type of bonus at a national level, total contracts written at a company level, and contracts written for specific subgroups (e.g., GAs—enlistment contracts where the individual has a high school diploma and scores at or above the fiftieth percentile on the AFQT) at a company level. In computing these measures, we again limit the sample to contracts written at centers with a nonzero contract mission in the 50 states or the District of Columbia with at least one recruiter on production at the recruiting center. This sample selection means that the model presented in Chapter Four relies on economic and demographic measures measured consistently in the 50 states and the District of Columbia.

Data on the total training seats planned for future months are collected from the accession mission letter issued by HQDA's ODCS G-1. The mission letter represents strategic guidance to USAREC and the Training and Doctrine Command reflecting the number of accessions they should plan by month during the fiscal year. The mission letter specifies quality and overall accession targets. Since the quality targets in the mission letter rarely change, we use only the accession mission. The mission letter is released at least once a year to set the next fiscal year targets. If the overall accession mission changes, or if projected accessions exceed or fall short of the original fiscal year targets, then a new mission letter may be released updating the monthly targets.

Television Advertising Data

Our analysis focuses on the resources exercised in the recruiting company area during a month and prior months (for resources with delayed effects). Data on advertising take three common forms—planned, purchased, and actual. Moreover, the date that payments are made may also differ from when the commercials are aired, based on the networks' billing cycles. Our analysis matches actual payments with the dates commercials are aired and the realized marketing impressions for the aired commercials measured by a third-party media analytics service. We worked with AMRG and the Army's advertising agency to collect this information for national TV advertising, which typically represents around 71 percent of media expenditures. National advertising differs from local advertising in that it is purchased through national media networks and these contracts guarantee a minimal number of national impressions achieved, but do not guarantee local impressions achieved. Both national and local TV advertising result in local impressions, but AMRG and the Army's ad agency use only national advertising.[2] With the focus on actual TV advertising cost, we exclude fixed costs associated with the Army's marketing contract, as well as costs associated with marketing events, local advertising, and internet advertising. These are not incorporated into our analysis due to lack of the required data.[3] We discuss the implications of this for the model and interpreting the model's results in Chapter Five.

We collect two types of TV advertising data: impressions and costs. Impressions are a function of gross rating points (GRP) and population size.[4] GRP is a measure of viewership and is collected in different

---

[2]   Occasionally, local TV advertising may be placed by a USAREC recruiting organization (i.e., battalion, company, or center), but data on impressions and spending are not available for this activity.

[3]   For these factors to systematically bias our results, they would have to be highly correlated with the use of the resources that we model: bonuses, recruiters, and TV prospect advertising. Decisions on local events and advertising are made by USAREC battalions or companies and are likely not coordinated with the advertising agency's national advertising campaign, or with enlistment incentives that are set nationally, or with recruiters, who are assigned based on persistent need. Therefore, it is unlikely that local event or advertising activity will bias our national resourcing measures. They could be used to explain additional unaccounted-for differences, however. Internet advertising could bias our measured estimates if the variation in use and geography were highly correlated with our resourcing measures in a causal way. Since both geographical and time variation would have to be highly correlated with internet advertising for this bias to occur, we believe that it is unlikely to be a major issue, but will pursue this question in future research.

[4]   That function is Impressions = (GRP/100) × Population Size. If an ad campaign results in 20 percent of the target seeing the advertising four times on average, then the campaign's size is 80 GRPs, or 0.8 impressions per person.

ways for each media market. Methods for measuring GRP include local people meter, set metered, and diary markets. Local-people-metered markets continuously collect viewership information from households where the meters have been installed and on the persons within them. Set-metered markets continuously collect information from households, and separate diaries of one week's viewing behavior for all individuals within a sample of households. Diary markets rely only on the one-week diaries for viewership behavior, and are more common in smaller media markets. Diaries are collected four times a year, in February, May, July, and November, also known as sweep periods. Continuous collection methods allow the third-party media analytics firm to project the number of national impressions from specific advertisements. The national impression measure can then be projected to the local level using person-based meters and diary-based measures.[5]

Projections to local media markets are not typically done, however. Dertouzos and Garber (2003) used data from the 1982–1984 Advertising Mix Test, which resulted in detailed local advertising data collection, to make such projections. As part of this research, we worked with AMRG and the Army's ad agency to do these projections based on the advertising that occurred during FY 2012–2015, which represents the longest period for which this level of detailed data have been collected. To make these projections, the ad agency used a tool provided by the third-party media analytics firm that distributes achieved national-level GRP to local media markets using the sweeps week measures in each fiscal year.[6] TV activity was based on and run against November sweep periods for FYs 2012, 2014, and 2015. For FY 2013, the February sweep period was used because the New York media market delivery was unavailable for November due to weather-related reasons. Each population has its own GRP measure. Target populations for Army advertising include prospects, defined as males aged 18–24, and influencers, all adults aged 35–54. For better accuracy, local impressions are

---

[5] Diary-based measures may be underreported or overreported due to recall error.

[6] Day parts were custom created according to individual fiscal years, but were limited to what was available within the tool's database (e.g., Discovery Military and Discovery Science were not available).

calculated by media market TV sizes for each target population specific to each fiscal year. The sizes of these populations are also measured during sweep weeks. The result is a monthly measure of TV advertising impressions by target population for each marketing area.

The Army ad agency provided data on actual monthly TV advertising costs. During this time period, the Army marketing plan included advertising targeted at prospect and influencer markets. In Figure 3.1, we demonstrate variation in ad spending during FY 2012–2015 based on the target audiences for the Army marketing plan.

Variation in advertising during this time frame was substantial, with advertising increasing during FY 2015 as the recruiting environment became more difficult. Advertising campaigns aimed at prospects reflect a mixture of advertisements aired on TV shows that appeal to the prospect population. It is possible for these campaigns to also generate influencer impressions. Analogously, the influencer campaigns reflect a mixture of advertisements aired on TV shows that appeal to the influencer population, but may yield a combination of prospect and influencer impressions. These campaigns have differing goals. A prospect campaign is aimed at generating awareness among potential recruits about an Army career, whereas an influencer campaign is aimed at generating awareness about the Army among a population that is largely ineligible to enlist. A potential by-product of an influencer's positive perception of the Army is that this individual might be more likely in the future to recommend or support the Army as a potential career option. Campaigns may not specifically target prospects or influencers; for example, if the objective were to improve the perception of the Army brand, that might result in a campaign targeted at the general adult population segment aged 18–49. The design of the campaign depends on the objective. One shortcoming of the impressions data provided by the Army's ad agency was that it did not separate prospect impressions by the prospect campaign versus the influencer campaign, or influencer impressions by the influencer campaign versus the prospect campaign.

Our objective in this research is to determine the optimal mix of recruiting resources to achieve annual accession and DEP goals. To do this, our analysis focuses on the resources exercised in the recruiting company area during a month and prior months (for resources with

Figure 3.1
Army TV Advertising Spending by Month (FY 2012–2015)

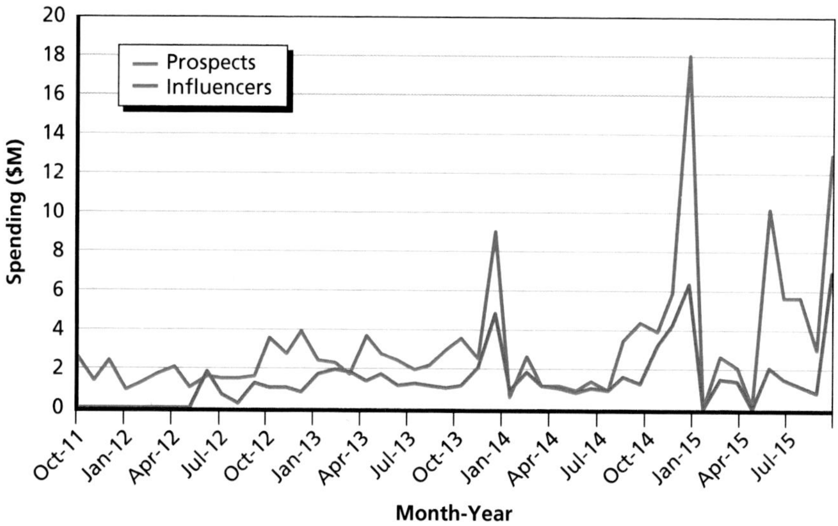

NOTE: Cost numbers based on data provided by the Army's ad agency reflecting actual monthly spending on advertising, distributed by advertising campaign type. Prospect advertising campaigns focus on a mixture of advertising that is attractive to males aged 18–24. Influencer advertising campaigns focus on a mixture of advertising that is attractive to adults aged 35–54.
RAND RR2364A-3.1

delayed effects). Given the different focuses of the prospect and influencer campaigns, our analysis uses only TV prospect impressions, as this campaign has the most direct theoretical effect on contract production. Additionally, we use TV advertising spending associated with the prospect advertising campaign in our analysis because this campaign by design influences immediate and near-term contract production.

Economic and Demographic Data

Since recruiting varies based on economic differences and population size, we incorporate economic and demographic factors into the model. We use the Woods and Poole projections of qualified military available by zip code based on U.S. Census population data as our main measure of the enlistment-eligible population. Qualified military available are defined as U.S. citizens 17–24 years of age who are eligible and available for enlisted military service without a waiver. Ineligibility is based on (1) medical/physical, (2) overweight, (3) mental health, (4) drugs, (5) conduct, (6) dependents, and (7) aptitude criteria.[7]

Unemployment rates are measured using the Current Population Survey, a household survey administered on a monthly basis by the U.S. Census Bureau, and reflect the official definition of unemployment for reporting purposes. The U.S. Bureau of Labor Statistics computes these measures and projects county-level unemployment rates on a monthly basis.

Remaining Technical Notes

In general, data were collected so that they would correspond to the recruiting resources, enlistment eligibility policies, and economic conditions in effect as of each calendar month from August 2002 through September 2015. This fully covers the Army's fiscal years from 2003 to 2016, as well as the last two months of FY 2002. However, not all data neatly correspond to calendar months. Contract-related measures correspond to recruiting contract months (RCMs), which typically run from the middle of the prior month to the middle of the current month (e.g., the May 2017 RCM runs from April 14 to May 11). Starting in 2014, USAREC changed this terminology to "phaseline"; however, we retain the original terminology in this report. Accession-related measures correspond to recruiting ship months (RSMs). The RSM ends on the last business day preceding the last Monday of the month, except

---

[7] Estimates of qualified military available are calculated by applying experienced rejection rates to military available from the geographical area using data from the National Health and Nutrition Examination Survey, National Survey on Drug Use and Health, Joint Advertising Market Research and Studies Youth Poll surveys, Military Entrance Processing Command Production Applicants AFQT Score Database, Woods and Poole Economics' Population Estimates, and the 1997 Profile of American Youth. (See Joint Advertising Market Research and Studies [2016].)

in September, when it corresponds to the last day of the fiscal year. The end of an RSM typically falls between the end of an RCM and the end of a calendar month. This difference in timing is unavoidable, as some measures are recorded using only one type of month measure. For example, contract mission is allocated only at the RCM level. Likewise, national economic measures are reported at the calendar-month level and typically reflect outcome measures from surveys administered over the course of that month. The modeling method described in Chapter Four considers a variety of specifications that account for lagged effects from key measures of broad economic and Army-specific data.

Recruiting Resource Model

The RRM developed in this chapter reflects the complex sequence of events associated with recruiting, represented in Figure 4.1. Resources and policies set by Army agencies produce contracts. DEP length affects a recruit's willingness to follow through with his or her contract. Who accesses determines costs through bonuses paid and the need to recruit additional people to replace the training seats for canceled contracts. Finally, economic factors may change the cost and rate of success in meeting the accession goal at multiple stages.

An early version of the RRM (Orvis et al., 2016) built on existing research to assess an optimal resource mix model. It focused on the same resources: recruiters, TV advertising, and enlistment incentives. It calibrated resource-productivity functions representing how resource levels relate to contract production based on previous estimates from the enlistment supply literature described in Chapter Two. Some of the measures were estimated over 30 years ago; for example, the last measures of enlistment incentive responsiveness or responsiveness to TV advertising were based on randomized controlled experiments (the gold standard of the program evaluation literature) from the early to mid-1980s. As described in Chapter Two, many studies since then have had the data necessary to measure responsiveness only for some resources. In particular, data on television advertising have been difficult to collect. Analyzing the enlistment responsiveness to advertising requires detailed data beyond what are typically collected by the Army. Measuring exposure to advertising in local markets is necessary to separate the relationship between enlistments and advertising exposure from factors correlated with national levels of advertising spending (e.g., spending on

Figure 4.1
Design of the RRM

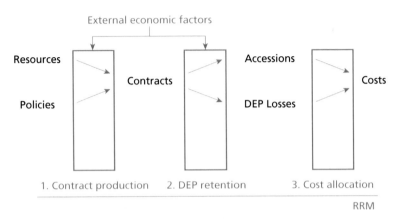

advertising is greater during difficult recruiting periods). What distinguishes the present work from the earlier model is that we update those earlier measures to reflect the recruiting environment in FY 2012–2015, collecting the data necessary to estimate a model capturing recruiters, TV prospect advertising, and enlistment incentives during the same period. We have made five key innovations since this past work. The first innovation is that enlistment incentives reflect alternative methods of use—MOS and quick-ship. As described in Chapter Two, the Army varied both the level and the eligibility for these bonuses over this time period. The second innovation was collecting the data for and estimating the S-curve for TV prospect advertising on a more recent sample. A third innovation was updating the contract production to reflect recent USAREC business practices, including team recruiting and assigning centers both RA and Army Reserve missions. The fourth innovation was to incorporate DEP attrition conditional on contract type and the scheduled DEP length. The fifth innovation was to develop the model at a monthly level, which links the timing of contract production with the scheduled training seats.

In this chapter, we discuss the three submodels of the RRM, represented in Figure 4.1. As part of the discussion of contract production, we discuss identification of the key model parameters and how they compare with past measures, and produce illustrations of the marginal responsiveness to each resource (all else equal).

Contract Production

Team-based recruiting was the primary recruiting method during FY 2012–2015. This means that a contract mission is allocated at the center or company level, and that success or failure is determined by the entire team's efforts in achieving the center's or company's contract goal (i.e., where the team is composed of the recruiters assigned to the center or company). Functionally, a mission is assigned to the company by the battalion, which has its mission assigned by its brigade leadership in consultation with USAREC.

The focus on recruiting teams alters the focal level of the analysis. Specifically, our unit of observation should reflect the level on which production takes place, so that the contract production function can represent the underlying mechanism that produces contracts. Our conceptual model is inspired by past work (Dertouzos and Garber, 2003); however, it makes the contract production function more explicit.

Before the model is described, a conceptual note. In developing this model, we theorize that the recruiter is the critical underlying resource needed to generate a contract. Regardless of how a potential recruit initially expresses interest (e.g., through GoArmy.com, at an event, showing up at a center), the center's recruiting team is responsible for meeting with the potential recruit, taking the interested recruit to the Military Entrance Processing Station for physical and aptitude testing, and interacting with him or her during the time between signing the contract and shipping to basic training. In fact, many recruiters maintain a relationship with their recruits for years to come. Thus, the number of recruiters in a recruiting team is the primary input in our specification, and other components augment the recruiting team's productive ability. Those other components may influence recruiter effort (e.g., eligible population, team mission) or increase the recruiting team's productive ability (e.g., number of days in a contracting month, the offering of a bonus, or advertising). However, if there were no recruiters, then our specification would predict zero contracts.

Theoretical Model

Let C_{st} represent the number of contracts written at company s in recruiting contract month t. Similarly, R_{st} represents the number of recruiters, M_{st} represents the mission at this company in this recruiting contract month, and P_{st} represents the number of qualified military available in the geographic area covered by the company in this month. The production of contracts at the company level is defined as

$$C_{st} = \left(R_{st}^{1-\alpha M - \alpha P} \cdot M_{st}^{\alpha M} \cdot P_{st}^{\alpha P} \right) \times$$
$$e^{\left(f_1(RE_t) + f_2(UE_{st}) + f_3(AD_{st}) + f_4(Bonus_t) + \beta X_{st} + \gamma_s + \varepsilon_{st} \right)}, \quad (4.1)$$

where

$f_1(RE_t)$ represents a nonlinear function of the national recruiting environment in month t

$f_2(UE_{st})$ represents a nonlinear function of the local unemployment rate in month t for company s's geographic area

$f_3(AD_{st})$ represents a nonlinear function of dollars spent targeting the relevant age group for prospective enlistees in month t for company s's geographic area

$f_4(Bonus_t)$ represents a nonlinear function for a vector of bonus-related variables, $Bonus_t$, that reflects the level and eligibility rate of bonuses at the national level

βX_{st} represents other factors augmenting production that vary by month and/or company, such as the number of days in month t available for signing a contract

γ_s represents a company-fixed effect that captures time-invariant factors during this time frame of analysis (which include educational composition of local area, propensity to serve in the local area, etc.)

ε_{st} represents unobserved transitory factors that could affect company s's contract-writing ability during month t, such that $\varepsilon_{st} \sim N\left(\beta_0, \sigma^2 \right)$.

This functional form has several interesting conceptual motivations. First, note that the core of the production function, $\left(R_{st}^{1-\alpha_M-\alpha_P} \cdot M_{st}^{\alpha_M} \cdot P_{st}^{\alpha_P} \right)$, relies on recruiters, mission, and the eligible population to be nonnegative in order to produce any contracts. Second, the functional form exhibits constant returns to scale, suggesting that if you doubled recruiters, mission, and the population, then contracts written would also double. Third, the functional form in Equation 4.1 represents a classical constant returns to scale Cobb-Douglas production function in economics, where recruiters, mission, and eligible population represent the main factors of contract production at the company level and the exponential term in Equation 4.1 reflects the technical efficiency of the company's production. The elements in the exponential term influence technical efficiency by making it easier or harder for recruiters to produce contracts (e.g., more advertising increases awareness among potential recruiters; higher unemployment rate means fewer employment options for the eligible population). Fourth, assuming $\alpha_P + \alpha_M \in (0,1)$ and $\alpha_P \in (0,1)$, then this production technology suggests diminishing returns from increasing only recruiters or contract mission. Conceptually, this says that adding recruiters and increasing contracting mission have a limited ability to produce further contracts without enlarging the eligibility base. Finally, if $\alpha_M, \alpha_P \in (0,1)$, the form $R_{st}^{1-\alpha_M-\alpha_P} \cdot M_{st}^{\alpha_M} \cdot P_{st}^{\alpha_P}$ highlights the trade-off between the number of recruiters in the field trying to sign contracts, represented by R_{st}, and recruiter effort. In this case, company mission, M_{st}, is a proxy for effort. In setting the mission, if the battalion could drive recruiters to be more productive without the need to increase the number of recruiters, then $\alpha_M = 1 - \alpha_P$. However, if inducing more effort by setting higher goals has a limit, then we would expect $\alpha_M < 1 - \alpha_P$. If the battalion cannot induce any additional effort (i.e., each additional recruiter will produce a set amount regardless of the missioning goals), then $\alpha_M = 0$. The results of previous research (Dertouzos and Garber, 2006) suggest that $0 < \alpha_M$, indicating that recruiting team effort plays an important role in overall production.

The nonlinear production function, Equation 4.1, can be transformed into a more estimable form by taking the logarithm of both sides and reorganizing R_{st}, resulting in the following:

$$\ln\left(^{C_{st}}/_{R_{st}}\right) = \alpha_M \ln\left(^{M_{st}}/_{R_{st}}\right) + \alpha_p \ln\left(^{P_{st}}/_{R_{st}}\right) + f_1(RE_t)$$
$$+ f_2(UE_{st}) + f_3(AD_{st}) + f_4(Bonus_t) + \beta X_{st} + \gamma_s + \varepsilon_{st}. \quad (4.2)$$

We can further define the structure of $f_2(UE_{st}) = \beta_{UE} \cdot \ln(UE_{st})$, $f_3(AD_{st})$, $f_3(AD_{st})$, $f_4(Bonus_t)$, and the elements of X_{st}. For the present analysis, we define $f_1(RE_t) = \beta_{RE,1} \cdot RE_t + \beta_{RE,2} \cdot RE_t^2 + \beta_{RE,3} \cdot RE_t^3$ so that national difficulty in recruiting can have increasing and diminishing effects. Additionally, we define $f_2(UE_{st}) = \beta_{UE} \cdot \ln(UE_{st})$, consistent with the past literature on enlistment contract supply. The resulting coefficient, β_{UE}, will represent the percentage change response of contracts per recruiter for a given percentage change in unemployment.

We define $f_3(AD_{st}) = \sum_{m=0}^{m=5} g(AD_{s,t-m})$, where $g(AD_{s,t-m})$ is defined as the S-curve of lag m, a functional form introduced by Dertouzos and Garber (2003) that represents the unique nature of advertising, where a little advertising has minimal effect, but as marketing saturation increases and individuals are exposed to promotional images of the Army, the returns to advertising increase. However, the S-curve also captures market saturation, whereby an additional dollar spent in a market with high exposure yields no additional contracts. The functional form of the S-curve is given by

$$g(AD_{s,t-m}) = \frac{\kappa_m}{1 + \exp\left(5 - \mu \cdot AD_{s,t-m}\right)}, \quad (4.3)$$

where $\kappa_m = \theta^m$ for $m \in [2,5]$, and the parameters κ_0, κ_1, θ, and μ are parameters to be estimated. The specification follows from Dertouzos and Garber (2003), where the specification for κ_m allows for delayed effects of TV advertising. Identification of the S-curve in Equation 4.3 relies on variation in television advertising impressions in the recruiting company area relative to other areas. TV advertising impressions vary significantly over FY 2012–2015 due in part to changes in funds allocated to TV advertising, but also due to geographic variation in TV viewership. To the degree that a company area is more likely to watch TV, we can exploit the variation in dollars spent per impression within a company area to identify the returns to advertising. Note that the effect of television advertising is assumed to be additive within the augmentation term, meaning that it is substitutable with other factors in this term (but not directly with recruiters or contract mission). It is also important to note that national advertising could be endogenous, meaning that it may be increased in response to poor aggregate recruiting conditions. Our setup, where the parameters of Equation 4.3 are identified using within-company variation in exposure to advertising, should reduce the likelihood of this bias since TV advertising is not changed in response to company-level recruiting conditions.

The bonus function is defined as $f_4\left(Bonus_t\right) = \beta_{BONUS,1} \cdot Bonus_t + \beta_{Bonus,2} \cdot Bonus_t^2$. The variable $Bonus_t$ reflects the principal component measure of quick-ship bonus eligibility, quick-ship bonus level, MOS bonus eligibility, and MOS bonus level. These variables are highly collinear. Rather than include these measures independently, we estimate a principal components factor model and extract the first principal component. This allows us to utilize the common variance of the economic indicators and use the factor weights to calculate the principal component measure of these four bonus factors.

Our measure of recruiter effort, as described above, uses contract missioning at the company level as a proxy. However, company-level recruiters may have competing demands for their time. First, it is generally perceived that meeting total mission is more important than meeting mission for specific quality types. Second, while our focus here has been on active component contracts, since FY 2012, USAREC centers and companies have been missioned to recruit across the Total Army (TA), which includes the RA and the USAR.[1] This means that a center may be tasked to recruit both active and reserve component contracts. Therefore, greater pressure through higher reserve component missioning may draw attention away from active component missioning. As a result, we redefine M_{st} to reflect this potential tradeoff:

---

[1]   The TA also includes the Army National Guard (ARNG); ARNG recruits its own force. We do not include ARNG in our analysis of USAREC recruiting.

$$M_{st} = \left(M_{st}^{RA}\right)^{\lambda_{RA}} \cdot \left(M_{st}^{TA}\right)^{\lambda_{TA}}, \qquad (4.4)$$

where we assume constant returns to scale ($\lambda_{RA} + \lambda_{TA} = 1$) and λ_{TA} will reflect the substitution or complementarity of the TA recruiting effort. If $\lambda_{TA} < 0$, then greater reserve component missioning reduces effort toward writing active component contracts. While we would expect active and reserve component contract writing to be substitutable, it is also possible that they are complementary ($\lambda_{TA} > 0$) if searching for individuals interested in the reserve actually reveals people interested in active service. Equation 4.4 causes Equation 4.2 to become

$$\ln\left(C_{st}^{RA}/R_{st}\right) = \tilde{\lambda}_{AC}\ln\left(M_{st}^{RA}/R_{st}\right) + \tilde{\lambda}_{TA}\ln\left(M_{st}^{TA}/R_{st}\right) + \alpha_p\ln\left(P_{st}/R_{st}\right)$$
$$f_1(RE_t) + f_2(UE_{st}) + f_3(AD_{st}) + f_4(Bonus_t)$$
$$+\beta X_{st} + \gamma_s + \varepsilon_{st}, \qquad (4.5)$$

where $\tilde{\lambda}_{RA} = \lambda_{RA} \cdot \alpha_M$ and $\tilde{\lambda}_{TA} = \lambda_{TA} \cdot \alpha_M$.

Finally, we will incorporate a number of factors as additional controls into our model through X_{st}. We incorporate as a control the number of days in a recruiting contract month. More days eligible for signing a contract means that more contracts can be signed (in this case, variation is only over time, not company). We also include indicators for each recruiting contract month to capture seasonal variation in contract write rates.

HQ enlistment contracts are typically a limiting factor in achieving annual accession goals. We hypothesize that resource responsiveness may be more limited for this particular type of contract, and it may be more sensitive to resource choices. We adapt the contract production model in Equation 4.1 to focus on HQ enlistment contracts. Specifically, Equation 4.4 is adapted to include HQ mission targets:

$$\tilde{M}_{st} = \left(M_{st}^{HQ}\right)^{\lambda_{HQ}} \cdot \left(M_{st}^{RA}\right)^{\lambda_{RA}} \cdot \left(M_{st}^{TA}\right)^{\lambda_{TA}}, \qquad (4.6)$$

where M_{st}^{HQ} is the HQ active component mission for the company in that RCM. We assume constant returns to scale ($\lambda_{HQ} + \lambda_{RA} + \lambda_{TA} = 1$)

and λ_{HQ} reflects the responsiveness to a greater relative HQ contract mission. Since M_{st}^{RA} equals the sum of HQ and non-HQ missions for the active component, there is an implied equivalence between HQ and non-HQ contracts in M_{st}^{RA}. Adding $\left(M_{st}^{HQ}\right)^{\lambda_{HQ}}$ allows the model to capture differences in the efficacy of additional HQ missions relative to any active missioning.[2] For example, if $\lambda_{RA} > 0$, then increasing the ratio of non-HQ to HQ missions results in greater HQ contract production. If true, this could reflect that greater effort at producing any contracts increases the probability of recruiters finding potential HQ enlistees. Additionally, $\widetilde{Bonus}_t$ is substituted for $Bonus_t$ and reflects the principal component measure of HQ quick-ship bonus eligibility, HQ quick-ship bonus level, HQ MOS bonus eligibility, and HQ MOS bonus level. Adapting Equation 4.5 to reflect these changes, the model for HQ contract production (C_{st}^{HQ}) in company s and RCM t becomes:

$$
\ln\left(C_{st}^{HQ}/R_{st}\right) = \tilde{\lambda}_{HQ}\ln\left(M_{st}^{HQ}/R_{st}\right) + \tilde{\lambda}_{RA}\ln\left(M_{st}^{RA}/R_{st}\right) + \tilde{\lambda}_{TA}\ln\left(M_{st}^{TA}/R_{st}\right)
$$
$$
+\alpha_P\ln\left(P_{st}/R_{st}\right) + f_1(RE_t) + f_2(UE_{st}) + f_3(AD_{st})
$$
$$
+f_4\left(\widetilde{Bonus}_t\right) + \beta X_{st} + \gamma_s + \varepsilon_{st}, \tag{4.7}
$$

where $\tilde{\lambda}_{HQ} = \alpha_m \cdot \lambda_{HQ}$.

Identifying Model Parameters

The parameters of the model in Equation 4.7 can be estimated on national data, but we choose to use company-level data instead. Our reason for using more granular data is concern regarding the

---

[2] A mathematical transformation of Equation 4.6 may be helpful for interpretability. Note that the active component mission is composed of HQ and non-HQ ($M_{st}^{RA} = M_{st}^{HQ} + M_{st}^{nonHQ}$) and that the TA mission is composed of the active and reserve components ($M_{st}^{TA} = M_{st}^{RA} + M_{st}^{RC}$). Extracting M_{st}^{HQ} from the last two elements of Equation 4.6 results in a function composed of the HQ mission and the ratio of other missions to the HQ mission:

$$
\tilde{M}_{st} = M_{st}^{HQ} \cdot \left(1 + M_{st}^{nonHQ}/M_{st}^{HQ}\right)^{\lambda_{RA}} \cdot \left(1 + M_{st}^{nonHQ}/M_{st}^{HQ} + M_{st}^{RC}/M_{st}^{HQ}\right)^{\lambda_{TA}}.
$$

endogeneity of resource decisionmaking. Endogeneity is where the outcome can influence the response. If the Army is resourcing to meet its accession mission, then the choice and level of resources will reflect what is required to achieve that mission. Consequently, we might observe a decrease in accessions from one year to the next, but an increase in bonus use. If the Army raised bonuses because it observed that recruiting difficulty was increasing, then a correlation between bonuses and accessions would yield a negative relationship. It is unlikely that bonuses would decrease enlistment. Instead, we would say that the estimate of the bonus parameter is biased, because the variation in the underlying data intended to capture the relationship between enlistments and bonuses is capturing another factor, such as recruiting difficulty.

To ensure that the estimated response to a resource is actually reflective of its productivity (and not the Army's response), we require measures on the right-hand side of Equation 4.7 that are independent of the outcome on the left-hand side. While this is easily true of external factors like unemployment rate or days in an RCM, resources are likely to be endogenous nationally. Resources assigned at the local level, while influenced at the margins by the local commander, are generally outside the local commander's control. Bonus eligibility and levels are determined nationally by the EIRB. Advertising buys are mostly determined and purchased nationally, while locally regions will differ in how much youth watch television. Even recruiter assignments, while potentially influenced by a local commander, are set by USAREC. Using local variation in resourcing requires that an estimated parameter, to be significantly different from zero, must demonstrate on average, across all companies, that a higher level of that resource (holding other measures on the right-hand side of Equation 4.7 constant) is consistently associated with a change (positive or negative) in the outcome on the left-hand side (i.e., HQ contracts). Additionally, long lead times for getting resources into the field due to the programming and recruiter assignment process reduces the likelihood that resources can be brought to bear on a local area within the month when need is anticipated by a local commander.

Even with these considerations, it is still possible that resources do have some residual endogeneity, and this will lead to bias in the parameter estimates. The potential for endogeneity should be kept in mind when interpreting our estimates.

Data and Estimation of HQ Contract Production

The data used to estimate Equation 4.7 come from the datasets described in Chapter Three. The data are aggregated to the recruiting-company level based on the recruiting station identification (RSID) code and the RCM. Recruiting stations (now called centers) within a recruiting company are included only if they have a mission including at least one HQ contract, have one or more recruiters on duty, and fall within one of the 50 states or the District of Columbia. Since nonrecruiting data (e.g., unemployment, TV advertising, and youth population) are not recorded by RCM, we lag these values by one month. For example, since the March RCM typically covers the last half of February and the first half of March, we assign nonrecruiting information from February to the March RCM. Additionally, nonrecruiting data are not provided for recruiting-company areas, so we translate the data into recruiting company areas using the zip codes of the RSID.

When data are not available at the zip code level, we generate an estimate of the nonrecruiting-level measure for the recruiting company area by reweighting the measure's level based on the 2010 Census population. For example, in the case of TV advertising, the data are reported at the designated marketing area (DMA) level. Consider the possibility of a recruiting company that has 60 percent of DMA A's population and 40 percent of DMA B's population based on the 2010 Census. To transform TV advertising impressions measured at the DMA level to the recruiting company level, we assume that TV advertising impressions are constant across the zip codes of the DMA. Consequently, the recruiting station's TV advertising impressions will reflect 60 percent of DMA A's TV ad impressions plus 40 percent of DMA B's TV ad impressions.

Table 4.1 represents the data used in estimating Equation 4.7 for two different time periods. The shorter time period represents the months for which we have TV advertising data on impressions and spending. We observe that lower average missions and fewer contracts characterize the more recent period, which reflects the lower accession goals during this time period. Average population is higher and unemployment varies less in the shorter, more recent time period. The average number of contracting days in an RCM is similar between time periods. Wenger et al.'s (forthcoming) measure of recruiting difficulty indicates that, on average, recruiting companies slightly exceeded their HQ contract goals during the more recent time period (e.g., a measure of 1.05 suggests that the moving average of national GA contract mission achievement was 5 percent above goal). The longer time period exhibits substantially greater variation in recruiting difficulty. Finally, enlistment bonus measures exhibit less variance in the recent time period, and are less broadly available for a given month.

Before estimating the model, we compute a latent bonus measure using factor analysis. Rather than include the measures for bonus level, eligibility, and type independently, we estimate a principal components factor model and extract the first principal component. This allows us to utilize the common variance across the different bonus measures. The resulting factor analysis and factor loadings are reported in Tables 4.2 and 4.3. In computing the factor analysis, we use the full time period we have available for these measures, August 2003–August 2015.

The results in Table 4.2 suggest that the factors load on a single common factor, judged by an eigenvalue exceeding one. Table 4.3 indicates that, for this factor, all four elements have significant importance, with quick-ship bonus measures being relatively more important than MOS bonus measures. The predicted bonus measure based on the first principal component ranges from a minimum of 0.33 to a maximum of 3.81, with a mean of 1.62 and standard deviation of 1.04 over the sample period. From January 2012 to August 2015, the mean is 0.91 with standard deviation of 0.30, reflecting the lesser use of incentives during this time period.

The model in Equation 4.7 is estimated using a nonlinear least squares estimator that accounts for company-level fixed effects using a

Table 4.1
Recruiting Company Descriptive Statistics for Samples Used in Contract Production Models—HQ

Variable	January 2012–August 2015				August 2003–August 2015			
	Mean	SD	Minimum	Maximum	Mean	SD	Minimum	Maximum
HQ RA NPS contracts	13	6	1	48	14	7	1	62
RA NPS contracts	22	10	1	82	25	11	1	97
On-production recruiters	30	8	8	60	32	9	1	68
HQ RA mission	18	6	1	47	19	7	1	54
RA mission	26	9	1	66	30	11	1	84
TA mission	32	10	7	75	38	13	6	102
Qualified military available population, ages 17–24	40,568	14,302	14,135	88,307	39,004	13,213	967	117,104
Unemployment rate	6.80	1.79	2.34	16.26	6.76	2.37	1.93	18.81
Contracting days in RCM	21	3	16	32	22	3	15	32
Ad spending ($1,000)	14	17	0	219	—	—	—	—
Recruiting difficulty measure (12-month moving average)	1.05	0.12	0.92	1.33	0.93	0.26	0.50	1.37
Latent bonus measure	0.91	0.30	0.41	1.63	1.62	1.04	0.33	3.81

Table 4.1—Continued

Variable	January 2012–August 2015				August 2003–August 2015			
	Mean	SD	Minimum	Maximum	Mean	SD	Minimum	Maximum
Bonus level conditional on receiving an MOS bonus, GAs	13,823	3,582	6,962	19,846	12,212	5,733	3,976	26,359
Percentage taking an MOS bonus, GAs	3.2	3.2	0.7	14.4	44.3	31.2	0.7	90.5
Bonus level conditional on receiving a quick-ship bonus, GAs	5,688	5,537	—	17,455	9,615	8,388	—	26,910
Percentage taking a quick-ship bonus, GAs	3.9	8.0	0.0	34.9	24.6	28.2	0.0	88.9
Sample size	8,877				33,936			

NOTE: Dashes indicate no bonus availability.

Table 4.2
Principal Component Analysis: Bonus Variables—Eigenvalues

Component	Eigenvalue	Difference	Proportion	Cumulative
Comp1	2.89	2.11	0.72	0.72
Comp2	0.78	0.58	0.20	0.92
Comp3	0.20	0.07	0.05	0.97
Comp4	0.13	—	0.03	1.00

Table 4.3
Principal Component Analysis: Bonus Variables—Factor Loadings

Variable	Comp1	Comp2	Comp3	Comp4
Bonus level conditional on receiving an MOS bonus, GAs	0.73	0.66	0.11	0.16
Percentage taking an MOS bonus, GAs	0.79	−0.57	0.02	0.21
Bonus level conditional on receiving a quick-ship bonus, GAs	0.93	0.08	−0.36	−0.09
Percentage taking a quick-ship bonus, GAs	0.94	−0.11	0.25	−0.22

within estimator.[3] Model 1 of Table 4.4 reports the estimated parameters using only January 2012–August 2015 company-level data.[4]

The results for Model 1 are generally intuitive. We observe that a greater population, higher unemployment, and more recruiting days in a month are associated with more HQ contracts. The parameters of the TV advertising response function (e.g., $\kappa_0, \kappa_1, \theta, \mu$) reflect the advertising S-curve, that is, $\kappa_0, \mu > 0$, $\theta \in (0,1)$. We estimate $\kappa_1 < 0$, which is unusual, but the estimate is not statistically different from zero. The results suggest that recruiting is associated with contracts in the month of the advertisement airing, but not with the month after, and that there is a notable delayed but diminishing effect of TV prospect advertising for two to five months after the advertising has aired. We find that $\tilde{\lambda}_{RA} > 0$, indicating that a larger RA mission, regardless of quality, has the potential to increase HQ enlistments in a recruiting company. Additionally, we find that $\tilde{\lambda}_{TA} < 0$, indicating that a larger USAR mission has the potential to decrease HQ enlistments in a recruiting company. Based on the economic model above, $\alpha_M = \tilde{\lambda}_{HQ} + \tilde{\lambda}_{RA} + \tilde{\lambda}_{TA} = 0.10$, which means that $\alpha_R = 1 - \alpha_M - \alpha_P = 0.24$, which means that greater HQ missions and more recruiters lead to more HQ contracts, albeit with diminishing returns to each.

One unintuitive relationship is $\tilde{\lambda}_{HQ} < 0$. The implication is that for a constant RA mission, a greater share of the overall mission focused

---

[3] Prior to estimating our model, we conducted an experiment to verify that the parameters of a hypothetical model resembling Equation 4.7 that included an S-curve and company-level fixed effects could be recovered using a nonlinear least squares estimation technique with a within estimator. The within estimator relates the variation in a company's resources over time with variation in its contract production. This experiment involved creating a synthetic dataset given a user-parameterized model with a prespecified number of companies, each with its own individual fixed effect, and differential exposure to advertising. Using our nonlinear least squares methodology, we were able to successfully recover the user-specified parameters. A similar methodology using maximum likelihood was inconsistent, likely because of the interactions between our nonlinear model and the optimization algorithm used by the maximum likelihood estimation algorithm.

[4] We did not use the first quarter of FY 2012 (October 2011–December 2011), because of incomplete advertising data. We did not use September 2015, because the contract data for this month were incomplete at the time our analytical dataset was produced.

Table 4.4
Contract Production Models—HQ, NPS

Time Period	Model 1 January 2012– August 2015	Model 2 August 2003– August 2015	Model 3 January 2012– August 2015
$\tilde{\lambda}_{HQ}$, mission (RA, HQ only)	−0.10** (0.05)	0.12*** (0.02)	−0.19*** (0.04)
$\tilde{\lambda}_{RA}$, mission (RA)	0.51*** (0.06)	0.29*** (0.02)	0.59*** (0.06)
$\tilde{\lambda}_{TA}$, mission (RA and USAR)	−0.31*** (0.07)	—	−0.24*** (0.07)
α_P, youth population	0.66*** (0.06)	0.38*** (0.01)	0.66*** (0.06)
β_{UE}, unemployment rate	0.20*** (0.06)	0.45*** (0.01)	0.30*** (0.05)
Days in RCM	0.03*** (0.002)	0.02*** (0.001)	0.02*** (0.001)
$\beta_{BONUS,1}$, latent bonus measure	−0.68*** (0.12)	0.26*** (0.02)	+
$\beta_{BONUS,2}$, latent bonus measure (squared)	0.30*** (0.06)	−0.05*** (0.004)	+
$\beta_{RE,1}$, recruiting difficulty measure	28.00* (16.99)	−3.75*** (0.46)	+
$\beta_{RE,2}$, recruiting difficulty measure (squared)	−19.88 (15.12)	5.54*** (0.52)	+
$\beta_{RE,3}$, recruiting difficulty measure (cubic)	4.27 (4.47)	−2.23*** (0.18)	+
κ_0	0.11*** (0.03)	—	0.12*** (0.03)
κ_1	−0.03 (0.03)	—	−0.03 (0.03)
θ	0.39*** (0.04)	—	0.40*** (0.04)
μ	4.83*** (0.49)	—	4.83*** (0.46)
October	0.17*** (0.03)	0.10*** (0.01)	0.13*** (0.02)

Table 4.4—Continued

Time Period	Model 1	Model 2	Model 3
	January 2012–August 2015	August 2003–August 2015	January 2012–August 2015
November	0.04	0.06***	−0.06**
	(0.02)	(0.01)	(0.02)
December	0.14***	0.09***	0.07***
	(0.02)	(0.01)	(0.02)
January (omitted)			
February	0.17***	0.08***	0.15***
	(0.03)	(0.01)	(0.02)
March	0.10***	0.00	−0.01
	(0.03)	(0.01)	(0.02)
April	0.17***	−0.01	0.04**
	(0.02)	(0.01)	(0.02)
May	0.19***	0.00	0.08***
	(0.02)	(0.01)	(0.02)
June	0.19***	0.00	0.08***
	(0.02)	(0.01)	(0.02)
July	0.12***	0.05***	0.05**
	(0.02)	(0.01)	(0.02)
August	0.10***	0.12***	0.03
	(0.02)	(0.01)	(0.02)
September	−0.02	0.05***	−0.04*
	(0.02)	(0.01)	(0.02)
Sample size (company-month obs.) R-squared	8,887 0.90	33,936 0.50	8,887 0.89

NOTE: All models reflect parameter estimates of Equation 4.7. Robust standard errors are in parentheses. Statistical significance of the parameter estimates is denoted by *** if $p<.01$, ** if $p<.05$, and * if $p<.1$. Models 1 and 3 are estimated using nonlinear least squares with a within estimator. Model 2 is estimated using ordinary least squares with a within estimator. Model 2 excludes a response function for both TV advertising (because data are unavailable before January 2012) and TA missioning (because team recruiting was not widely done before 2012). The latent bonus measure is computed from the principal component analysis discussed in the text, and the recruiting difficulty measure reflects the 12-month moving average of the GA mission achievement ratio. The marker "+" indicates that Model 3 imposes the parameter estimates from Model 2.

on HQ production reduces a recruiter's HQ production. We discuss potential rationale for this estimate after introducing and reporting the results of Models 2 and 3.

As part of Model 1, we incorporated a latent bonus measure based on principal component analysis that reflected the common variation between eligibility and bonus levels for quick-ship and MOS bonuses (similar to the analysis reported in Tables 4.2 and 4.3). However, the estimated parameters in Model 1 reflect a negative association between bonuses and HQ enlistments over a low range of the latent bonus measure (it is positive at high ranges of the bonus measure). This suggests the counterintuitive result that more bonuses (e.g., either through greater bonus eligibility or through high bonus levels) result in fewer HQ contracts over this lower range. This likely reflects the use of bonuses when recruiting is difficult, leading to an endogeneity problem. This point is further discussed below.

Additionally, we estimated the response to the 12-month moving average of Wenger et al.'s (forthcoming) measure of recruiting difficulty. Their measure of recruiting difficulty was the mission attainment for HQ contracts, so the 12-month average reflects persistent, recent past difficulty in achieving HQ contract mission.[5] The estimated parameters suggest little responsiveness to this measure of recruiting difficulty between 80 and 120 percent HQ contract mission attainment, which is the region for which this measure is available during the January 2012–August 2015 time period.

Given the limited time frame, it is possible that the key national measures, particularly bonuses, are not identified independently of contemporaneous Army responses to the recruiting environment. Past research has noted that parameters for recruiting resources can be biased because the Army increases their use in response to difficult recruiting conditions. The design of the model provides for geographic and time variation in TV prospect advertising and recruiters, allowing for identification of these parameters based on within-company variation over time. The identification of the national-level bonus and recruiting dif-

---

[5] This measure is not endogenous, because it reflects the previous 12-month HQ mission attainment at the national level.

ficulty measures is based on common national differences independent of the other factors (e.g., if bonus eligibility is expanded, then all recruiting companies should exhibit a common, proportionate increase in HQ contract production). During Model 1's limited time frame, bonuses were most heavily used in mid-2015, as the recruiting environment was worsening, likely leading to the unintuitive result and conflating changes in recruiting difficulty with bonuses.

We address this issue by estimating the model in Equation 4.7 over a longer time period, August 2003–August 2015. This requires excluding the response function for TV prospect advertising due to lack of data. We also omit a measure for TA contract mission since the time frame largely reflects a period before RA recruiters were writing USAR contracts.[6] The results are presented in Model 2 in Table 4.4. In this model, the parameters of both national level measures—the latent bonus measure and recruiting difficulty—reflect logical functional relationships within the observed ranges. The latent bonus measure exhibits diminishing returns. The measure of recruiting difficulty exhibits an S-curve relationship over the observable ranges of the difficulty measures. Specifically, the effect of difficulty plateaus below between 0.45 and 0.50 and above between 1.15 and 1.20, with an inflection point between 0.85 and 0.90. Intuitively, these measurements suggest that in very difficult (easy) recruiting environments, a worsening (improving) recruiting environment will not have a substantial negative (positive) effect on HQ contract production. However, an improvement in the recruiting environment between 0.5 and 1.2, characterized by an increasing level of the recruiting difficulty measure, yields substantial increases in HQ contract production. We will discuss the translation between these measures and predicted changes in HQ contracts later in this chapter.

Briefly we also consider some relative comparisons between the common parameters estimated across Models 1 and 2. In the broader time period, the role of population, α_p, was less important in overall company HQ contract production, as the coefficient decreased from 0.66

---

[6]   In additional model runs incorporating the TA mission, we found similar parameter estimates. Results are available from the authors upon request.

to 0.38. The role of recruiter effort, $\alpha_M = \tilde{\lambda}_{HQ} + \tilde{\lambda}_{RA} + \tilde{\lambda}_{TA} = 0.41$, increased substantially, and the role of the number of recruiters in a company decreased slightly, $\alpha_R = 1 - \alpha_M - \alpha_P = 0.21$.[7] The change may be attributable, in part, to the switch from individual-level to center-level missioning. Additionally, the association between the local unemployment rate and contract production was larger in the broader time frame (0.45 versus 0.20), and the association between days in an RCM was similar across the two models.

Since the objective of this work is to produce a contract production model that accounts for sensitivity to different recruiting resources, we impose the national-level response functions estimated on August 2003–August 2015 data on Equation 4.7 and reestimate Model 1. This reflects a strong assumption that responsiveness to these national-level measures is constant over time.[8] Later in this chapter, we compare resources' responsiveness with previous estimates and find that response rates to national-level bonuses are consistent with past estimates, and that the responsiveness to recruiting difficulty is intuitive.

---

[7] We set $\tilde{\lambda}_{TA} = 0$ in Model 2 since this encompasses a time period when USAREC did not mission RA recruiters with a USAR mission.

[8] In Equation 4.1, the recruiting company's innate productivity is determined by $\left(R_{st}^{1-\alpha_M-\alpha_P} \cdot M_{st}^{\alpha_M} \cdot P_{st}^{\alpha_P} \right)$. This innate productivity is augmented by the factors in the exponential term, which include the national measure of recruiting difficulty and the national bonus measure. Because these measures are captured only at the national level, looking at only four years provides limited variation by which to identify their response (as highlighted by the odd results in Model 1). This is what motivated our estimation of Model 2. Imposing the response to these measures on Model 3 reflects a strong assumption that how these measures augment a company's productivity remains constant. We recognize that this is a strong assumption, and later in this chapter we will compare the responsiveness of these elements with other measures and compare the nonimposed measurements with their earlier estimates. As we highlight later in the chapter, we find that the bonus elasticity is similar to previous measures, and that the recruiting difficulty measure reflects a reasonable pattern of responsiveness (this is in lieu of a comparison since there are not previous results to compare with). We see two alternatives to imposing these parameters. The first would be to impose parameters (i.e., calibrate) based on previous estimates. The second would be to exclude these factors from the contract production model. Neither of these is appealing relative to our chosen method, since the first would omit the recruiting difficulty measure, and the second would omit a resource (i.e., bonuses) that past estimates suggest expands contract production and for which the Army invests significant funds with the expectation that it expands the market.

We refer to the new model as Model 3. Comparing Models 1 and 3, we observe that the local youth population remains an important determinant of HQ contract production. The role of contract missioning increases in relative importance compared with the number of recruiters, $\alpha_M = 0.16, \alpha_R = 0.18$. Additionally, HQ contract production becomes relatively more responsive to local unemployment compared with Model 1, and the associations of days in the RCM and seasonality are largely the same. In terms of the response function for TV prospect advertising, the parameter estimates do not meaningfully change.

Model 3 again reflects the unintuitive relationship: $\lambda_{HQ} < 0$. This negative effect is not desirable, because it implies that for a constant RA mission, a greater share of the overall mission focused on HQ production led to a decrease in HQ production. To understand the potential drivers of this relationship, we calculated two ratios: the monthly ratio of HQ mission to overall contract mission and the monthly ratio of HQ contracts to overall contract production. Ratios are chosen because they are independent of the recruiting mission and contract magnitudes. When the HQ mission/Overall RA mission ratio was plotted over time, it ranged between 0.6 and 0.7 in most years from 2002 through 2015. The HQ contract/Overall RA contract ratio declined from the first quarter of FY 2012 to the second quarter of FY 2014, dropping from 0.61 to 0.56. At the same time, the HQ mission/Overall RA mission rose from 0.63 to 0.74. This relationship is reflected in the regression parameters, where $\tilde{\lambda}_{HQ} < 0$. As mentioned, this negative effect is not desirable. A plausible inference is that the programming and allocation of recruiting resources did not keep pace with the changing recruiting environment and mission. If resourcing had been adequate and responsive to conditions, we might have expected no decrease in the HQ contract/Overall RA contract ratio.

We consider a few potential theoretical rationales for $\tilde{\lambda}_{HQ} < 0$. One is that missioning a larger share of overall RA contract production for HQ encourages recruiters to pursue strategies that limit overall production, which incidentally leads to lower HQ contract production. Recruiters do not know with certainty whether an individual is HQ until after interacting with him or her (at least for determining whether he or she has a high school diploma) or until the potential recruit visits a military entrance processing station to take the AFQT (although recruiters can give potential recruits a preliminary test like the AFQT during an interaction before the Military Entrance Processing Station). An example might help illustrate the potential mechanism. A recruiter tasked with a larger fraction of HQ might set up a booth at a community college instead of at a jobs center. The recruiter's motivation for doing this is that he or she expects the rate of HQ individuals to be greater at the community college. If the rate of potential interest in the Army is substantially greater at the latter than at the former, then it is possible that the overall HQ production may decrease.

An alternative explanation for this result is endogeneity. It is possible that after a period of sustained success, company leadership establishes greater quality goals. If recruiters respond to a post-successful period by reducing effort, then the simultaneous actions of the leadership and recruiting force could generate this association.

There is notable variation within Table 4.4 between the relative importance of α_M and the direction of $\tilde{\lambda}_{HQ}$. In Model 2, $\tilde{\lambda}_{HQ} > 0$, and the relative importance of missioning, α_M, is greater than in Models 1 and 3. We do not know what drives the difference in mission-based productivity, or the sign reversal between Model 2 and Models 1 and 3. One possibility is that starting in FY 2012, USAREC changed its business practices toward team recruiting. As discussed in the text, this meant that recruiting centers, not individual recruiters, were held accountable for contract production. Around the same time, these centers were also made responsible for the USAR mission. The dynamics of how the change in USAREC business practices might affect the measured response of α_M and the direction of $\tilde{\lambda}_{HQ}$ are not clear. Similar parameters in past work that specifically address how a greater fraction of HQ missions is related to HQ contract production do not exist. Dertouzos and Garber (2008) examine a switch from individual to team recruiting from 1999 to 2001. They find that team recruiting is associated with greater production, except in particularly easy or particularly difficult recruiting environments. This suggests that missioning and environment may interact in a nonlinear way that is not captured by the theoretical model presented above. The easier recruiting environment of FY 2012–2015 (as compared with the whole of FY 2003–2015) could result in a downward bias for α_M. It is possible that $\tilde{\lambda}_{HQ} < 0$ represents a transitional effect in FY 2012–2015 reflecting a period when recruiting conditions were relatively more favorable, and may reverse signs as more data become available.

The most important component from the modeling perspective is the overall response to mission, α_M. When we operationalize the contract production function at the end of this chapter, the contract production model does not permit the reallocation of local contract missions between HQ and non-HQ, or between RA and USAR. It only allows for changes in the overall mission rate per recruiter. An evaluation of how changes in USAREC business practices alter productivity is outside the scope of this report. This report uses estimates based on the more recent time period.

For the rest of this report, we consider Model 3 in Table 4.4 to be our HQ contract production model.

Illustration and Comparison of HQ Contract Production's Resource Response Functions

The model parameters presented in Table 4.4 are not directly comparable with the past estimates of HQ contract production's responsiveness to recruiting resources and environment. To facilitate this comparison, we use the observed values of resources and the other model inputs for FY 2014, and then consider variation in predicted contract production based on variation in one input while the other inputs are held constant. The responsiveness of HQ contract production to this input can then be measured and compared with past estimates.

First, we consider the responsiveness with respect to advertising. The ninety-ninth percentile of company-level advertising expenditure translates to approximately $19.7 million in monthly national-level TV prospect ad spending. Figure 4.2 reports annual HQ production numbers predicted by our contract production model for constant monthly ad spending between $0 and $19.7 million (or up to $236 million in annual TV prospect ad spending). Additionally, we use the structure of the model to predict out the productive ability of TV prospect advertising spending up to $360 million (indicated by a dashed blue line). To compare this with previous estimates, we impose Dertouzos and

Figure 4.2
HQ Contract Production Response to TV Prospect Advertising

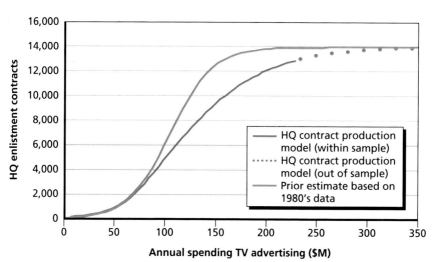

NOTE: HQ production model estimates, both in and out of sample, correspond to HQ contract production predictions using Model 3 of Table 4.4 and holding other resources in FY 2014 constant. Estimates of the TV advertising response function are from Orvis et al. (2016) and are based on Dertouzos and Garber (2003) estimates using the Advertising Mix Test results from the mid-1980s. Orvis et al. (2016) update this response function to 2012 based on adjustments for overall inflation (Consumer Price Index–Urban Consumers [CPI-U]) as measured by the U.S. BLS, inflation in advertising expenditures, and changes in the youth population level. For the purposes of this comparison, we further inflated these values to 2014 dollars using BLS's CPI-U. In all cases, the monthly national TV expenditure is held constant. The prior estimates do not distinguish between influencer and prospect TV advertising, whereas the response function in Model 3 of Table 4.4 is limited to only TV prospect advertising (i.e., advertising impressions for males aged 18–24).

RAND RR2364A-4.2

Garber's (2003) estimates of the S-curve in 2014 dollars. We find that the response function for TV prospect advertising indicates (1) that TV advertising continues to be an important recruiting lever for the Army, and (2) while TV advertising is less effective at lower expenditure levels than in past estimates, it still reflects an S-curve that exhibits threshold and saturation levels for TV ad spending.

Next, we consider the response to the number of recruiters. When adjusting the number of recruiters in Model 3 of Table 4.4, we assume the recruiters are increased or decreased proportionately across recruiting companies.[9] Increasing recruiters can be sensitive to how contract missioning is adjusted in response. We consider three cases: missions do not increase as recruiters increase, missions increase by existing mission ratios within each company, and missions increase by twice the existing mission ratios within each company. For example, if in a recruiting company the ratio of HQ contract missions to recruiters is 1 and the average RA mission to recruiters ratio is 2, then if an additional recruiter is added to the company, missions will increase by 1 and 2, respectively. We include the "twice the existing mission ratios" case because it reflects that missioning changes can outpace recruiter changes when the recruiting objectives are changing, resulting in an above-unit-average change in contract missions. Table 4.5 presents estimates of the percentage change in HQ enlistment contracts relative to the percentage change in recruiters at specific recruiter levels (i.e., elasticity). Estimated elasticity ranges from 0.15 to 0.60, depending on assumptions regarding contract missioning and the number of recruiters. Since changes in recruiter levels are generally associated with changes in missioning, we would expect our elasticity to fall somewhere between the last two columns' levels in Table 4.5 for the given number of recruiters. Past work from the post-1990s military drawdown has found recruiter elasticities that range from 0.41 to 0.63 (Asch et al., 2010; Asch, Hosek, and Warner, 2007), with the exception of Dertouzos and Garber (2003), who find an elasticity of 0.11. Comparing the results in Table 4.5 with these past results, our estimated recruiter elasticities for a missioning change equal to the company's existing mission to recruiter ratios are somewhat lower than those in previous reports. This could reflect the move to team recruiting, differences in recruiter motivation over time, or other factors affecting recruiter productivity.

---

[9]   It is possible that recruiters are inefficiently allocated across companies. While the contract production function we estimate in Model 3 of Table 4.4 could be used to determine an efficient reallocation of recruiters, it is outside the scope of the present work.

Table 4.5
HQ Contract Production Response to Recruiters

Recruiters	No Change in Mission with Each Additional Recruiter	Missioning Change Equal to Company's Existing Mission to Recruiter Ratios	Missioning Change Equal to Twice Company's Existing Mission to Recruiter Ratios
	Elasticity	Elasticity	Elasticity
5,500	0.15	0.37	0.60
6,000	0.15	0.36	0.56
6,500	0.16	0.36	0.52
7,000	0.16	0.36	0.50
7,500	0.16	0.36	0.48
8,000	0.16	0.36	0.46
8,500	0.16	0.36	0.45

The response function for enlistment incentives is often difficult to identify because enlistment incentive policy is typically implemented uniformly across the country, and incentives are generally used when recruiting conditions are difficult, biasing the effect downward. A recent estimate of enlistment bonus elasticity was 0.17 by Asch et al. (2010), which is a high level of responsiveness compared with previous measurements. Most post-drawdown measures of bonus responsiveness range from 0.05 to 0.12 (Asch, Hosek, and Warner, 2007). Our results may differ from these analyses, which typically exploit variation at the state or Military Entrance Processing Station geographical level, in that (1) our geography more closely mirrors the Army recruiting enterprise's business model, which missions at the nearly 240 recruiting company level and below, (2) we use national bonus values (i.e., average national bonus take rates and levels) to proxy for bonus eligibility rather than the values for the contracts signed within a particular geography, and (3) we use a latent bonus measure capturing the common variance in bonus eligibility, levels, and types. The most scientifically rigorous assessment of bonus elasticity, specifically dealing with the bonus level offered for a fixed eligibility level, was made as part of the Enlistment Bonus Experiment that took place in the early 1980s (Polich, Dertouzos, and Press, 1986). In this case, the authors found a bonus elasticity of between 0.07 and 0.08. Our estimates are reported in Tables 4.6 and 4.7. The estimates in Table 4.6 reflect the expansion of a $12,000 MOS or quick-ship bonus to a growing pool of eligible training seats for which a potential enlistee may choose to sign up. Quick-ship bonuses are estimated to be slightly more productive than MOS bonuses for HQ contracts. Estimated elasticities range from 0.02 to 0.11. Both bonus types exhibit diminishing returns. When MOS and quick-ship bonuses are increased in tandem, the point of diminishing returns occurs sooner due to substitutability between the bonus types.

Table 4.7 presents similar measures of the HQ contract production's response to increases in enlistment bonus levels. We find that HQ contract production increases with increasing bonus levels and that, similar to expanding eligibility, increasing bonus levels for both bonus types exhibits increasing responsiveness at low levels of bonuses, but diminishing at high levels. The results in Table 4.7 are most analogous to those in the Enlistment Bonus Experiment. The experiment fixed the MOSs eligible for bonuses and allowed the bonus level to differ between specific recruiting areas and length of enlistment contract. In the Enlistment Bonus Experiment, the control group was offered a $5,000 MOS bonus (equivalent to about $12,000 in today's dollars) and the first experimental group was offered an $8,000 bonus for the same MOS and same four-year contract length (equivalent to about $20,000). The second experimental group was offered either an $8,000 bonus for the same MOS and same four-year contract length or a $4,000 bonus for a three-year contract length for the same MOS. HQ enlistments into the eligible MOS represented just under 30 percent of all HQ enlistments during the baseline (preceding) year (see Table 3 of Polich, Dertouzos, and Press [1986]). Our estimates in Table 4.7 of $12,000 and $20,000, respectively, suggest that our measured bonus elasticity is greater than earlier estimates, but in the same relative region as the Enlistment Bonus Experiment and past measures of bonus responsiveness.

These measures of bonus elasticity are closely related to the concept of economic rent, which in the present context means the fraction

Table 4.6
HQ Contract Production Response to Enlistment Incentive Eligibility

Eligibility (%)	Expansion of $12,000 MOS Bonus Eligibility	Expansion of $12,000 Quick-Ship Bonus Eligibility	Expansion of $12,000 MOS and Quick-Ship Bonus Eligibility
	Elasticity	Elasticity	Elasticity
10	0.02	0.02	0.03
20	0.03	0.04	0.05
30	0.05	0.06	0.06
40	0.06	0.08	0.06
50	0.07	0.09	0.06
60	0.08	0.10	0.04
70	0.09	0.11	0.02
80	0.10	0.11	−0.01

NOTE: When considering one bonus type, the other bonus type is assumed to have a zero bonus level and eligibility. The results presented here are mainly intended to provide the reader with a sense of the potential range of elasticities, which is important for comparing them with previous estimates. Within a given column, elasticities may increase due to a high initial baseline level of production; for example, an increase from 30,000 to 31,000 HQ contracts is a small percentage change relative to the 50 percent increase of expanding eligibility from 20 to 30 percentage points. The initial increase followed by a decrease in elasticity of expanding eligibility for both bonuses is reflective of sharper diminishing returns and is not indicative that expanding both results in lower production. See Table A.1 for additional discussion relating to Table 4.6.

of additional bonus dollars paid to recruits who would have enlisted without the additional bonus dollars. Using our estimated elasticity of 0.09 for $12,000 and 30 percent eligibility from Table 4.7, this means that increasing the bonus level by 10 percent would yield only 0.9 percent more HQ enlistment contracts, indicating that over 90 percent of the additional dollars paid go to enlistees who would have signed a contract without the increase in the bonus. Even for the most general measures of elasticity from the past literature, the implied economic rent from bonuses is above 80 percent. This does not mean that enlistment

Table 4.7
HQ Contract Production Response to Enlistment Incentive Levels

Average Bonus Level ($)	Increase in MOS Bonus Level with 30% Eligibility	Increase in Quick-Ship Bonus Level with 30% Eligibility	Increase in MOS and Quick-Ship Bonus Level with 30% Eligibility
	Elasticity	Elasticity	Elasticity
4,000	0.04	0.03	0.05
8,000	0.07	0.06	0.09
12,000	0.09	0.08	0.10
16,000	0.11	0.10	0.09
20,000	0.13	0.11	0.05
24,000	0.13	0.12	0.00

NOTE: When considering one bonus type, the other bonus type is assumed to have a zero bonus level and eligibility. The results presented here are mainly intended to provide the reader with a sense of the potential range of elasticities. See note below Table 4.6 for additional detail on interpretation.

bonuses are an inefficient recruiting resource; it just means that the cost per contract from additional dollars spent is far greater than the face value of the bonus offered.

Data and Estimation of RA Contract Production

In an earlier version of the RRM, non-HQ enlistment contracts were assumed to be a fixed proportion of overall contracts, and HQ contract production could be traded for non-HQ contract production in a formulaic way that was independent of resource levels (Orvis et al., 2016). However, recruiting resources may act disproportionately on non-HQ contracts. Consider enlistment incentives. Since the determination of HQ is based on test scores and educational attainment, it is likely that non-HQ enlistees have fewer outside options, making enlistment a comparatively better option and requiring lower enlistment incentives. Operationally, the Army recognizes this, limiting enlistment incentives for non-HQ and often offering a lower incentive level. As an alternative to a formulaic trade-off between HQ and non-HQ contracts, we instead

estimate Equation 4.5 for all RA contracts. Potential non-HQ contract production is then treated as the difference between the estimate
version of Equation 4.5 and Equation 4.7. Realized non-HQ contract
production will depend on the Army's willingness to accept non-HQ
based on operational targets. We will discuss how this is incorporated
into the RRM later in this report, but first we follow a similar path to
our description of the HQ contract production function: describing
the underlying data, demonstrating the principal component analysis
for bonuses, and comparing reported estimates of Equation 4.5 for the
more recent and the broader time period.

The data used to estimate Equation 4.5 are the same as those
used to estimate Equation 4.7, with a slightly more expanded sample
reflecting that we restrict the sample to only companies composed of
centers with a mission of at least one RA contract (as opposed to at least
one HQ RA contract). Table 4.8 represents the data used in estimating Equation 4.5 for two different time periods. As before, we observe
that lower average missions and fewer contracts characterize the more
recent period, which reflects the lower accession goals during this time
period. Average population is higher and unemployment varies less
in the shorter, more recent time period. The average number of contracting days in an RCM is similar between time periods, and the
longer time period exhibits substantially greater variation in recruiting difficulty. Finally, enlistment bonus measures exhibit less variance
in the recent time period and are less broadly available for a given
month. Comparing GA with non-HQ enlistment incentives, we find
that bonus eligibility is lower for non-HQ contracts. Surprisingly, for
the broader time period, the average bonus level for non-HQ is slightly
greater than for GA contracts. This surprising relationship is due to
more restricted offering of non-HQ enlistment incentives (non-HQ
MOS bonus eligibility averaged 9 percent for this period versus 44
percent for GAs). Finally, in the recent time period, almost no non-HQ
MOS bonuses have been offered.

Before estimating the model, we again compute a latent bonus
measure using factor analysis. This time, we account for non-HQ bonus
eligibility, levels, and type in addition to GAs. The resulting factor
analysis and factor loadings are reported in Tables 4.9 and 4.10. In com-

Table 4.8
Recruiting Company Descriptive Statistics for Samples Used in Contract Production Models—All RA Contracts

Variable	January 2012–August 2015				August 2003–August 2015			
	Mean	SD	Minimum	Maximum	Mean	SD	Minimum	Maximum
HQ RA NPS contracts	13	6	1	48	14	7	1	62
RA NPS contracts	22	10	1	82	25	11	1	97
On-production recruiters	30	8	8	60	32	9	1	68
HQ RA mission	18	6	1	47	19	7	1	54
RA mission	26	9	1	66	30	11	1	84
TA mission	32	10	7	75	38	13	6	102
Qualified military available population, ages 17–24	40,568	14,302	14,135	88,307	39,004	13,213	967	117,104
Unemployment rate	6.80	1.79	2.34	16.26	6.76	2.37	1.93	18.81
Contracting days in RCM	21	3	16	32	22	3	15	32
Ad spending ($1,000)	14	17	0	219	—	—	—	—
Recruiting difficulty measure (12-month moving average)	1.05	0.12	0.92	1.33	0.93	0.26	0.50	1.37
Latent bonus measure	0.91	0.30	0.41	1.63	1.62	1.04	0.33	3.81

Table 4.8—Continued

Variable	January 2012–August 2015				August 2003–August 2015			
	Mean	SD	Minimum	Maximum	Mean	SD	Minimum	Maximum
Bonus level conditional on receiving an MOS bonus, GAs	13,823	3,582	6,962	19,846	12,214	5,733	3,976	26,359
Percentage taking an MOS bonus, GAs	3.2	3.2	0.7	14.4	44.4	31.2	0.7	90.5
Bonus level conditional on receiving a quick-ship bonus, GAs	5,688	5,537	—	17,455	9,617	8,387	—	26,910
Percentage taking a quick-ship bonus, GAs	3.9	8.0	0.0	34.9	24.6	28.2	0.0	88.9
Bonus level conditional on receiving an MOS bonus, non-HQ	12,040	12,112	—	40,000	12,540	8,321	—	40,000
Percentage taking an MOS bonus, non-HQ	0.1	0.1	0.0	0.6	9.2	15.1	0.0	74.3
Bonus level conditional on receiving a quick-ship bonus, non-HQ	2,951	4,458	—	13,527	7,161	7,079	—	26,000
Percentage taking a quick-ship bonus, non-HQ	2.1	7.1	0.0	35.2	14.4	18.6	0.0	54.8
Sample size	8,912				33,959			

Table 4.9
Principal Component Analysis: Bonus Variables for All RA Contracts—
Eigenvalues

Component	Eigenvalue	Difference	Proportion	Cumulative
Comp1	4.93	3.84	0.62	0.62
Comp2	1.10	0.39	0.14	0.75
Comp3	0.71	0.25	0.09	0.84
Comp4	0.45	0.02	0.06	0.90
Comp5	0.43	0.23	0.05	0.95
Comp6	0.20	0.08	0.02	0.98
Comp7	0.12	0.05	0.01	0.99
Comp8	0.06	—	0.01	1.00

puting the factor analysis, we use the full time period we have available for these measures, August 2003–August 2015.

The results in Table 4.9 suggest that the factors load primarily on a single common factor, but that there is a second important common factor, judged by an eigenvalue exceeding one. Table 4.10 indicates that for the first common factor, seven of the eight elements have significant importance, with quick-ship bonus measures being relatively more important than the MOS bonus measures. The bonus level of a non-HQ MOS bonus takes on notably less importance than the other seven measures. The predicted bonus measure based on the first principal component ranges from a minimum of 0.25 to a maximum of 3.53, with a mean of 1.42 and standard deviation of 1.02 over the sample period. From January 2012 to August 2015, the mean is 0.68 with standard deviation of 0.28, reflecting the lesser use of incentives during this time period. For consistency with our HQ contract production model, we use only the first principal component.[10]

---

[10] The second principal component in Table 4.10 reflects a trade-off between MOS bonus levels and eligibility. During FY 2003–2012, bonus levels were raised in tandem with eligibility. However, the second component is likely capturing that MOS bonus levels grew more

Table 4.10
Principal Component Analysis: Bonus Variables for All RA Contracts—Factor Loadings

Variable	Comp1	Comp2	Comp3	Comp4	Comp5	Comp6	Comp7	Comp8
Bonus level conditional on receiving an MOS bonus, GAs	0.68	0.45	−0.50	0.16	0.13	0.19	−0.03	0.07
Percentage taking an MOS bonus, GAs	0.79	−0.37	0.34	−0.06	−0.15	0.29	0.04	0.07
Bonus level conditional on receiving a quick-ship bonus, GAs	0.90	−0.03	−0.26	−0.24	−0.01	0.00	0.20	−0.13
Percentage taking a quick-ship bonus, GAs	0.93	−0.05	−0.01	0.12	−0.24	0.00	−0.22	−0.12
Bonus level conditional on receiving an MOS bonus, non-HQ	0.24	0.86	0.43	−0.06	−0.10	0.01	0.04	−0.02
Percentage taking an MOS bonus, non-HQ	0.77	−0.11	0.29	0.17	0.53	−0.02	−0.01	−0.04
Bonus level conditional on receiving a quick-ship bonus, non-HQ	0.87	0.01	−0.02	−0.44	0.06	−0.17	−0.10	0.10
Percentage taking a quick-ship bonus, non-HQ	0.87	−0.07	0.01	0.36	−0.20	−0.23	0.11	0.08

The model in Equation 4.5 is estimated using a nonlinear least squares estimator that accounts for company-level fixed effects using a within estimator. Model 1 of Table 4.11 reports the estimated parameters using only January 2012–August 2015 company-level data.

We follow a methodology for estimating Equation 4.5 that is similar to the methodology we followed for estimating Equation 4.7, and the results are similar. Given the similarity between the procedures, we highlight here only key differences. The parameters of the TV advertising response function (i.e.., $\kappa_0,\kappa_1,\theta,\mu$) reflect the advertising S-curve, that is, $\kappa_0,\kappa_1,\mu > 0$, $\theta \in (0,1)$. In the HQ contract production function, we found $\kappa_1 < 0$, but not statistically different from zero.

As with the HQ contract production function, the national-level measures produced odd results, so we addressed this issue by estimating the model in Equation 4.5 over a longer time period, August 2003–August 2015. The results are presented in Model 2 in Table 4.11. In this model, the parameters of the latent bonus measure exhibit diminishing returns. The measure of recruiting difficulty exhibits an S-curve relationship over the 0.60 and 1.15 ranges of the difficulty measures. Specifically, the effect of difficulty plateaus below between 0.60 and 0.65 and above between 1.10 and 1.15, with an inflection point between 0.90 and 0.95. Unlike the HQ contract production model, extreme values of recruiting difficulty show an odd pattern that likely reflects the Army's operational response under these circumstances. At levels of difficulty below 0.6, the response function sharply increases, while at levels above 1.15, it sharply falls. This pattern likely reflects that in these extreme circumstances, the Army loosens or tightens recruit eligibility requirements to meet accession goals. Namely, when the ratio is low, eligibility is increased to help ensure meeting overall RA production goals. Thus, the measure of RA production (vs. HQ production) relative to recruiting difficulty spikes up. Conversely, when GA production is high, the Army tightens eligibility to further increase recruit quality, and thus the

---

quickly than expanding eligibility, particularly during difficult recruiting times. Figure 2.3 provides an illustration for GA MOS contracts. Our interpretation of this is that it is more likely a structural Army response rather than a labor supply response, which is an additional motivation for its exclusion from the contract production model.

Table 4.11
Contract Production Models—All RA Contracts

Time Period	Model 1 January 2012– August 2015	Model 2 August 2003– August 2015	Model 3 January 2012– August 2015
$\tilde{\lambda}_{RA}$, mission (RA)	0.39*** (0.04)	0.35*** (0.01)	0.40*** (0.04)
$\tilde{\lambda}_{TA}$, mission (RA and USAR)	−0.26*** (0.05)	—	−0.22*** (0.05)
α_P, youth population	0.63*** (0.05)	0.43*** (0.01)	0.62*** (0.05)
β_{UE}, unemployment rate	0.32*** (0.05)	0.36*** (0.01)	0.42*** (0.04)
Days in RCM	0.02*** (0.001)	0.02*** (0.001)	0.02*** (0.001)
$\beta_{BONUS,1}$, latent bonus measure	−0.71*** (0.06)	0.14*** (0.01)	+
$\beta_{BONUS,2}$, latent bonus measure (squared)	0.49*** (0.04)	−0.01*** (0.003)	+
$\beta_{RE,1}$, recruiting difficulty measure	122.90*** (14.00)	−5.36*** (0.35)	+
$\beta_{RE,2}$, recruiting difficulty measure (squared)	−106.36*** (12.36)	6.53*** (0.39)	+
$\beta_{RE,3}$, recruiting difficulty measure (cubic)	30.42*** (3.62)	−2.45*** (0.14)	+
κ_0	0.19*** (0.03)	—	0.16*** (0.02)
κ_1	0.02 (0.02)	—	0.01 (0.02)
θ	0.51*** (0.02)	—	0.43*** (0.02)
μ	4.70*** (0.25)	—	5.83*** (0.35)
October	0.19*** (0.02)	0.14*** (0.01)	0.17*** (0.02)
November	0.03 (0.02)	0.09*** (0.01)	−0.02 (0.02)

Table 4.11—Continued

Time Period	Model 1 January 2012– August 2015	Model 2 August 2003– August 2015	Model 3 January 2012– August 2015
December	0.12*** (0.02)	0.07*** (0.01)	0.09*** (0.02)
January (omitted)	—	—	—
February	0.16*** (0.02)	0.08*** (0.01)	0.12*** (0.02)
March	0.09*** (0.02)	0.04*** (0.01)	0.04** (0.02)
April	0.17*** (0.02)	0.02*** (0.01)	0.13*** (0.02)
May	0.20*** (0.02)	0.03*** (0.01)	0.15*** (0.02)
June	0.12*** (0.02)	0.04*** (0.01)	0.12*** (0.02)
July	0.08*** (0.02)	0.07*** (0.01)	0.09*** (0.02)
August	0.07*** (0.02)	0.12*** (0.01)	0.06*** (0.01)
September	0.01 (0.02)	0.09*** (0.01)	0.00 (0.02)
Sample size (company-month obs.) R-squared	8,912 0.79	33,959 0.61	8,912 0.78

NOTE: All models reflect parameter estimates of Equation 4.5. Models 1 and 3 are estimated using nonlinear least squares with a within estimator. Model 2 is estimated using ordinary least squares with a within estimator. Model 2 excludes response function for both TV advertising (because data are unavailable before January 2012) and TA missioning (because team recruiting was not widely done before 2012). The latent bonus measure is computed from the principal component analysis discussed in the text, and the recruiting difficulty measure reflects the 12-month moving average of the GA mission achievement ratio. The marker "+" indicates that Model 3 imposes the parameter estimates from Model 2.

overall production measure falls relative to recruiting difficulty. Later on, we will discuss how these pressures will be handled in the RRM.

As before, we impose the parameters for the national-level response functions and reestimate Model 1. These results are presented in Model 3 in Table 4.11. Imposing the national-level parameters does not meaningfully alter the other parameters in Model 1. Briefly, we consider some relative comparisons between the common parameters estimated across Models 2 and 3. In the broader time period, the role of population (α_P) was less important in overall company contract production (as it was for the HQ contract production function), as it decreased from 0.63 to 0.43. The role of recruiter effort ($\alpha_M = \tilde{\lambda}_{RA} + \tilde{\lambda}_{TA}$) increased substantially in the broader time period from 0.13 to 0.35, and the role of the number of recruiters in a company ($\alpha_R = 1 - \alpha_M - \alpha_P$) decreased slightly from 0.24 to 0.22. As before, we note that this change may be attributable, in part, to the switch from individual-level to center-level missioning. An evaluation of how changes in USAREC business practices alter productivity is outside the scope of this report.

For the rest of this report, we consider Model 3 in Table 4.11 to be our RA contract production model.

Illustration and Comparison of HQ and RA Contract Production's Resource Response Functions

The enlistment supply literature focuses on HQ contracts, so there are no direct comparisons for the RA contract production model as there were for the HQ contract production model. Instead, we present the comparison of the RA and HQ contract production's responsiveness to recruiting resources. Theoretically, non-HQ enlistees should be more responsive to recruiting resources, holding all else constant, as they have fewer outside options and are typically demand constrained. Consequently, our comparisons between the two production functions should exhibit a greater relative responsiveness to resources for the RA production function.

Figure 4.3 compares HQ with RA contract production for specific levels of annual TV prospect advertising. At every level, the responsiveness of RA contract production to TV advertising is substantially greater.

Figure 4.3
RA and HQ Contract Production Response to TV Prospect Advertising

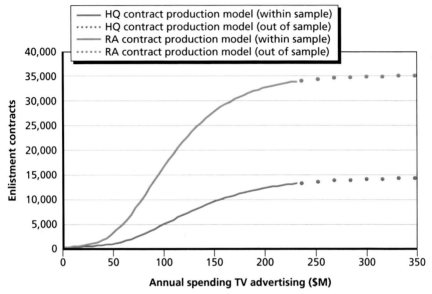

NOTE: HQ production model estimates, both in and out of sample, correspond to HQ contract production predictions using Model 3 of Table 4.4 and holding other resources in FY 2014 constant. Similarly, RA production model estimates, both in and out of sample, correspond to RA contract production predictions using Model 3 of Table 4.11 and holding other resources in FY 2014 constant. In all cases, the monthly national TV prospect advertising expenditure is held constant.
RAND RR2364A-4.3

    In Tables 4.12–4.14, we consider responsiveness to recruiters and enlistment incentives. The RA contract production model finds elasticities generally 0.01 to 0.03 greater for recruiters relative to the measured recruiter elasticities for HQ contract production (see Table 4.5). For enlistment bonuses, increases in quick-ship or MOS bonus eligibility increase elasticities by up to 0.02, while increases in bonus levels typically have somewhat lower responsiveness compared with the HQ contract production model (see Table 4.7). These results suggest that for HQ contracts, the offer of an enlistment incentive may be particularly salient in the enlistment decision and that it is easier for recruiters to produce non-HQ contracts, all else equal.

Table 4.12
RA Contract Production Response to Recruiters

Recruiters	No Change in Mission with Each Additional Recruiter	Additional Missioning Equal to Company's Existing Mission to Recruiter Ratios	Additional Missioning Equal to Twice Company's Existing Mission to Recruiter Ratios
	Elasticity	Elasticity	Elasticity
5,500	0.16	0.39	0.65
6,000	0.16	0.39	0.60
6,500	0.17	0.39	0.56
7,000	0.17	0.39	0.54
7,500	0.17	0.39	0.52
8,000	0.17	0.39	0.50
8,500	0.17	0.39	0.49

Operationalizing the Contract Production Models in the RRM

In the RRM, the contract production model is the framework by which the relative values of resources are compared. It links the use of a specific resource to overall and HQ contracts generated by that resource. The other two components of the RRM, namely, the DEP retention and cost allocation models, allow contracts and resources to be linked back to accessions and costs. Accessions and recruit quality are the two main goals of the recruiting enterprise, and the objective of the RRM is to help military planners accomplish these goals at minimal cost.

The previous analysis suggests that our HQ and RA contract production models act in sensible ways. For the HQ contract production model, our comparisons with past studies also suggest that our estimated response rates for different recruiting resources fit well with prior estimates, with the advantage of the present models being that they reflect the shift in focus of contract production from the recruiter to the recruiting center, reflect a longer recruiting history experience, and capture the three key recruiting resources in a common modeling framework.

Table 4.13
RA Contract Production Response to Enlistment Incentive Eligibility

Eligibility (%)	Expansion of $12,000 MOS Bonus Eligibility	Expansion of $12,000 Quick-Ship Bonus Eligibility	Expansion of $12,000 MOS and Quick-Ship Bonus Eligibility
	Elasticity	Elasticity	Elasticity
10	0.02	0.02	0.03
20	0.04	0.04	0.06
30	0.06	0.06	0.09
40	0.07	0.07	0.11
50	0.09	0.08	0.12
60	0.10	0.10	0.13
70	0.11	0.11	0.13
80	0.12	0.12	0.12

NOTE: Expansion in bonus eligibility is done evenly for HQ and non-HQ contracts. When considering one bonus type, the other bonus type is assumed to have a zero bonus level and eligibility. The results presented here are mainly intended to provide the reader with a sense of the potential range of elasticities. See note below Table 4.6 for additional detail on interpretation. A key difference in this result as compared with Table 4.6 is that the simultaneous expansion of eligibility for both incentives is associated with an increasing elasticity. This reflects that the growth rate of RA production remains relatively high even at high bonus offerings. Expansion of eligibility still exhibits diminishing returns, however.

To operationalize the use of the contract production model, we need to make several assumptions regarding how the RRM will use it, and about the relationship between contract production and recruit eligibility policies, such as HQ targets, enlistment waiver rates, and number of enlistments permitted among former service members (prior service recruits).

Since the contract production models are at the company level, and there are on average around 236 companies per month, a complete analysis would require specifying HQ, RA, and USAR mission, recruiters, the local unemployment rate, local exposure to advertising, and contracting days in a month for every recruiting company. This level of

Table 4.14
RA Contract Production Response to Enlistment Incentive Levels

Average Bonus Level ($)	Increase in MOS Bonus Level with 30% Eligibility	Increase in Quick-Ship Bonus Level with 30% Eligibility	Increase in MOS and Quick-Ship Bonus Level with 30% Eligibility
	Elasticity	Elasticity	Elasticity
4,000	0.01	0.02	0.03
8,000	0.03	0.04	0.06
12,000	0.04	0.06	0.08
16,000	0.06	0.08	0.10
20,000	0.07	0.10	0.12
24,000	0.08	0.11	0.12

NOTE: Expansion in bonus eligibility is done evenly for HQ and non-HQ contracts. When considering one bonus type, the other bonus type is assumed to have a zero bonus level and eligibility. The results presented here are mainly intended to provide the reader with a sense of the potential range of elasticities. See note below Table 4.6 for additional detail on interpretation. A key difference in this result as compared with Table 4.6 is that the simultaneous expansion of eligibility for both incentives is associated with an increasing elasticity. This reflects that the growth rate of RA production remains relatively high even at high bonus offerings. Expansion of bonus levels still exhibits diminishing returns, however.

detail would be too onerous for an analyst and would delay the quick analysis of resourcing trade-offs this research aims to provide. Therefore, we use FY 2014 as our baseline, as it reflects the last, full fiscal year of our estimation sample. We assume that changes in recruiting resources and environments are distributed to the company level based on company-to-national ratios in FY 2014. For example, if the unemployment rate increases by X percent, then we assume that the unemployment rate in the local area also increases by X percent. If recruiters are increased nationally, then the increase in recruiter levels is distributed proportionately across the country. For missioning, we assume missioning increases as recruiters are added in proportion to the company's existing mission to recruiter ratio in FY 2014. This point is important, because we are implicitly assuming that additional recruiter productivity is not

achieved through increased recruiter effort. This assumption is necessary because increased effort is costless in the context of a resourcing
model. Additionally, the contract production model does not permit the
reallocation of local contract missions between HQ and non-HQ, or
between RA and USAR. Advertising dollars are distributed to the local
level based on the companies' imputed share of overall TV prospect
viewership. Finally, contracting days in each RCM are assumed to be
the same as in FY 2014. These assumptions can be changed, and they
can be updated as additional years of data become available.

Once the inputs to the contract production model are chosen, the
production models produce monthly predictions for RA and HQ contracts. Potential non-HQ contracts correspond to the difference between
these two values. If the production of non-HQ contracts exceeds the
target non-HQ contracting rate, then the excess non-HQ contracts are
not signed. Conceptually, this reflects that the Army is selective and
regulates how many non-HQ contracts are produced.

We operationalize changes in the waiver rates by increasing the
number of contracts produced by proportionate deviations from the
historical waiver rate (calibrated to 11.7 percent, the waiver rate during
this time period). Mathematically, postwaiver contract levels are determined by

$$C_{post} = C_{pre} \cdot \left(\frac{1 - w_{historical}}{1 - w_{target}} \right),$$

where $w_{historical}$ is the historical waiver rate for the period the contract
production models are estimated and w_{target} is the target number of
waivers chosen by the analyst.[11] Waiver rates are assumed to influence

---

[11] Let $C_{post} = C_{pre} + w_{target} \times C_{post} - w_{historical} \times C_{pre}$. Then, $C_{post} \times (1 - w_{target}) = C_{pre} - w_{historical}$
$\times C_{pre}$, and $C_{post} \times (1 - w_{target}) = C_{pre} \times (1 - w_{historical})$. This means that $C_{post} = C_{pre} \times (1 - w_{historical}) / (1 - w_{target})$. Intuitively, this relationship expands contract production in a
fixed proportion relative to the historical level. For example, if the historical waiver
rate was 10 percent during the period when the contract production function was
estimated, and the Army expanded the percentage of waivers to 20 percent, then the
function would increase production by $(1 - 0.1) / (1 - 0.2) = 1.125$, which corresponds
to a production increase of 12.5 percent. This form assumes that the historical waiver

both HQ and non-HQ production proportionately. If the target waiver rate exceeds the historical waiver rate, the number of contracts produced increases; if the target waiver rate is below the historical waiver rate, it will reduce the number of contracts produced.

Finally, since the contract production models reflect NPS production, prior service contracts are produced based on target prior service accessions and these contracts are uniformly distributed across the RCM within the fiscal year. The target HQ contracting rate determines the proportion of HQ versus non-HQ prior service contracts.

The contract production model takes the following as inputs: resourcing levels, eligibility policy (i.e., target HQ percentage, waiver rates, prior service accession targets), recruiting environment (i.e., unemployment rate and the recruiting difficulty measure from Wenger et al. [forthcoming]), and the observed distribution of recruiting companies, recruiters, advertising exposure (the ratio of company-area impressions relative to national impressions), and local unemployment rates observed in FY 2014. The contract production model's outputs are the number of contracts produced by type (i.e., HQ or non-HQ) and with or without a quick-ship bonus.

DEP Retention Model

Once contracts are produced by the contract production function, they are assigned a DEP length based on existing training seat vacancies. The distribution of training seats reflects the distribution of target HQ contracts and is scaled to reflect the accession goals. While the enlistee is waiting to access, he or she has a probability of canceling the enlist-

---

rate is already reflected in the contract production function and that an expansion or contraction of the waiver rate has an effect on contract production that is independent of recruiting resources. In essence, we are assuming these contracts are demand constrained—they are ready and willing to enlist only if the Army accepts them. In extreme cases, for examples beyond waiver rates observed in recent history (a bit over 20 percent for our sample period), this assumption may not be valid. If the contracts produced through waivers were not demand constrained, then the contract production function would predict more contracts are produced than in reality.

ment contract. The DEP retention model captures the probability of contract cancelation between the month the contract is signed and the month that the recruit is scheduled to access.

Contracts produced from the contract production model are categorized by quick-ship and non-quick-ship bonuses, which will have different DEP schedules. HQ contracts can be either GA or senior alpha contracts, with the key distinction being that senior alpha contracts are scheduled for longer DEP times (hence are not eligible for quick-ship bonuses) and have different attrition rates. Senior alpha contracts are assumed to be a fixed proportion of HQ contract production. We use the historical rate of 21 percent from Orvis et al. (2016). We do not distinguish between senior and nonsenior contracts for non-HQ.[12]

DEP schedules (i.e., the months a contract is scheduled to be in the DEP) and attrition rates differ by the following five categories:

1.   GA contracts with a quick-ship bonus
2.   GA contracts without a quick-ship bonus
3.   Senior alpha contracts without a quick-ship bonus
4.   Non-HQ contracts with a quick-ship bonus
5.   Non-HQ contracts without a quick-ship bonus.

The original DEP schedules for each category are assigned based on a parameterized distribution. We begin with the distribution of DEP schedules available in FY 2014. These distributions for the three accession categories (i.e., GAs, senior alphas, and non-HQ) are presented in Table 4.15. However, recognizing that these distributions are long relative to historical averages, we shorten the average DEP length to 70 days (i.e., 2.3 months), as presented in the last two columns of Table

---

[12] The DEP retention model does not track the month of contract production. Consequently, senior alpha contracts are not necessarily assigned to access in the summer months. Additionally, senior non-HQ contracts are not separated from other non-HQ contracts. We do not anticipate that this has a notable impact on the outcome of the model, as senior alpha contracts and GA contracts fill similar HQ training seat requirements (i.e., the model does not consider the difference between senior alpha and GA contracts when judging whether accessions are achieving quality requirements). These simplifications reduce the computational complexity of the model but could be amended in future iterations.

4.15. The DEP retention model schedules non-quick-ship contracts to training seats based on the original distribution for senior alphas, and the new distributions for GA and non-HQ contracts. The DEP retention model considers attrition rates (Table 4.16) and the distribution of training seats when assigning contracts a scheduled DEP length. If the training seats in a specific accession month are filled sufficiently to account for attrition, then the scheduled DEP length of contracts is extended to the earliest month where a vacancy exists. For example, if a contract is written in January and would normally be scheduled to access in March, but March's training seats are full, then the contract is written for April. Consequently, while Table 4.15 reflects the starting distribution of scheduled DEP lengths, the realized distribution may be longer depending on training seat vacancies. Quick-ship bonuses are typically written for DEP lengths of 30 days or less, although these bonuses are occasionally used for DEP lengths of 31–60 days as well. We parameterize our starting quick-ship DEP length distributions to place 90 percent of contracts in DEP for one month or less (i.e., not more than 30 days) and 10 percent of contracts in DEP for between one and two months (i.e., 31–60 days). As with non-quick-ship bonuses, if training seat vacancies do not exist in a given month, then the scheduled DEP length is extended. In Table 4.15, the average DEP length for each range of days is shown in months (e.g., the average for 1–30 days is less than one month, the average for 31–60 days is one month, and so forth).

Once a contract is assigned a scheduled DEP length, the contract progresses through the DEP. Each month, the contract has a random probability of being canceled. We calibrate the DEP retention model using FY 2014 contract cancellation rates based on months scheduled to be in the DEP. The cumulative attrition rates (i.e., the probability of ever canceling a contract) from this time period are presented in Table 4.16 by scheduled DEP length. Generally speaking, the longer a contract is scheduled to be in the DEP, the more likely it will be canceled. Deviations from this trend in Table 4.16 are generally due to small sample sizes. Additionally, most contracts are canceled in the last two months before the recruit is scheduled to access. This could be due to either the recruit delaying the decision or the recruiter giving the recruit more time to reconsider. Regardless, the results presented in Table 4.16 indicate

Table 4.15
Starting Distribution of DEP Length by Accession Category

Months Scheduled to Be in DEP	% of GAs (Original)	% Senior Alphas (Original)	% Non-HQ (Original)	% GAs (New)	% Non-HQ (New)
Less than 1 month	2	0	1	8	12
1	16	0	8	24	27
2	24	1	21	29	32
3	31	4	28	21	12
4	19	12	19	12	8
5	3	12	6	2	2
6	2	10	3	2	1
7	2	11	3	1	1
8	1	11	3	0	1
9	1	11	2	0	1
10	0	5	1	0	0
11	0	8	2	0	1
12	0	6	1	0	1
13	0	6	1	0	0
14	0	2	0	0	0
Average months in DEP	2.9	7.7	3.9	2.3	2.3

that this is an important factor to account for, particularly at the end of the fiscal year. Entry pools for the next fiscal year that have longer average scheduled DEP lengths may require additional contracts to be written to compensate for the higher DEP attrition.

Operationalizing the DEP Retention Model in the RRM

In the RRM, the DEP retention model is the framework by which contracts fill training seats and how the RRM accounts for contract cancellations. To operationalize the use of the DEP retention model, we need

Table 4.16
DEP Attrition by Accession Category and Scheduled DEP Length

Months Scheduled to Be in DEP	% of GA Cumulative Attrition	% of GA Attrition Occurring in Two Months Before Ship Date	% of Senior Alpha Cumulative Attrition	% of Senior Alpha Attrition Occurring in Two Months Before Ship Date	% of Non-HQ Cumulative Attrition	% of Non-HQ Attrition Occurring in Two Months Before Ship Date
Less than 1 month	3	100	+	+	3	100
1	4	100	13	100	4	100
2	5	86	4	100	6	89
3	7	80	9	90	7	82
4	8	79	8	87	9	80
5	13	84	12	85	11	83
6	10	89	13	84	16	88
7	12	79	14	87	17	86
8	14	78	16	69	17	80
9	15	76	18	75	18	75
10	24	38	16	81	21	69
11	15	75	17	77	24	80
12	21	100	21	64	24	65
13	+	+	22	74	25	71
14	+	+	22	60	21	68

NOTE: Cumulative attrition reflects the percentage of contracts that are ever canceled. The marker "+" corresponds to a category with a sample size of zero (see Table 4.15), and hence could not be calculated. Because the sample size is zero, it will never be populated in the RRM. The rates for cells with non-zero sizes represent raw rates. We could have used a smoothing function to deal with small cell sizes at the higher values of months scheduled in the DEP, but chose not to do so because of the trivial impact of the small cells on our calculations.

to make several assumptions regarding how the RRM will use it, and the relationship between scheduling and training seats. Additionally, we need to assign contracts that are in the entry pool (i.e., contracts that exist at the beginning of the year) to existing training seats.

In reality, training seats are associated with a specific vacancy in an MOS training program. Whether a recruit is HQ may determine his or her eligibility for certain MOSs and hence eligibility for certain training seats. MOS eligibility characteristics and the timing of MOS training programs are determined by the needs of the Army. However, specifying every MOS's vacancy levels, timing, and eligibility criteria would result in a level of detail that would be too onerous for an analyst and would delay the quick analysis of resourcing trade-offs this research aims to provide. We simplify this process by making assumptions regarding the typical distribution of DEP lengths, and make the DEP retention model flexible enough to extend contract lengths as necessary based on training seat vacancies. As discussed, we use FY 2014 for parameterizing the DEP length distributions, as it reflects the last, full fiscal year of our estimation sample, but we shorten the average DEP length to reflect a lower operational bound. We set this value at 70 days (2.3 months) to reflect the generally perceived notion that shorter average DEP length needs to be incentivized through quick-ship bonuses.[13]

Another issue is how contracts in the entry pool for the current year are to be assigned to quality levels and DEP lengths given that they were produced outside the contract production model. Ideally, we would know their remaining DEP length and their distribution of quality. However, this information is not typically provided for the entry pool—simply the number of recruits is provided—and would be onerous for the analyst to calculate from the contract records database. Consequently, we simplify this process by assuming that the entry pool is composed of fixed GA, senior alpha, and non-HQ percentages (36.35 percent, 19.30 percent, and 44.45 percent, respectively), with a fixed number of months they each have remaining in the DEP (based

---

[13] This is not to suggest that quick-ship bonuses are required to get a recruit to ship within 60 days (in fact, Table 4.15 suggests that many recruits do so without these incentives), but that these bonuses are necessary to achieve an average DEP length below two months.

on Orvis et al. [2016]). We use FY 2014 contract cancellation rates based on months scheduled to be in the DEP to impute a distribution for how many months the contracts were originally scheduled for. For example, for GA contracts with one month remaining in the DEP at the beginning of the fiscal year, we impute a value for what fraction of those contracts had a DEP length of one month, two months, and so on. Based on the results in Table 4.16, if an entry pool is composed more heavily of contracts signed with longer DEP lengths, then more contracts are likely to be canceled in the current fiscal year.

The DEP retention model takes the following as inputs: the output of the contract production model; a user-specified training seat distribution, accession goal, target HQ accession percentage, and entry pool size; and the calibrated measures described above using observed FY 2014's distribution of DEP length and DEP attrition rates. Variation in external economic conditions influences DEP retention because higher rates of contract production during particularly good recruiting conditions result in longer DEP lengths (and hence greater attrition). The DEP retention model's outputs are accessions by month of the fiscal year and by type (e.g., HQ or non-HQ), the number of contracts in the DEP for the next year (i.e., entry pool for next fiscal year), and the number of eventual accessions by type for contracts signed in the current fiscal year.

Cost Allocation Model

Resourcing costs are allocated to the month a resource is used. For advertising, this corresponds to the month the advertising originally airs. For recruiters, we follow HQDA guidance and allocate a constant recruiter annual cost of $118,000 per year, or about $9,800 per month.[14] The recruiter cost reflects the number of recruiters on production in a month times the cost per recruiter. Finally, bonus costs reported in the model reflect obligations made during the fiscal year. These costs are

---

[14] This value was provided to RAND by HQDA.

based on the contracts that access since bonuses are not paid for canceled contracts.[15]

The cost allocation model takes the following as inputs: (1) the resourcing levels used in the contract production model, and (2) the current and future fiscal year accessions produced from those resources to determine the bonus costs. The cost allocation model's outputs are the total resourcing cost commitment by month for each of the resources.

RRM Validation

The complex sequence of steps represented by Figure 4.1 and discussed over the course of this chapter makes it important to validate the model to ensure it can accurately reproduce observed results for key outcomes of interest. As described above, the appropriate advertising data were made available for FY 2012–2015; this limited our validation to FY 2013–2015 since the model must account for lagged effects of advertising.[16] The RRM has been adapted into a software program that can be run by an analyst who specifies the following inputs:

- Size of the entry pool
- Recruit eligibility policy (waiver rate, HQ rate, number of prior service accessions)

---

[15] This likely reflects an overestimate for realized costs for the accessions during a given fiscal year. This is because bonuses up to $10,000 are paid upon completion of IET, and IET attrition is around 12 percent historically. Moreover, remaining payments for bonuses greater than $10,000 are paid out in equal installments ("anniversary payments") throughout the recruit's term of enlistment. Attrition over the first term averages 30–35 percent, historically. At the same time, however, anniversary payments needing to be made to past years' recruits are not currently included in the RRM. Including anniversary payments would increase realized costs. Given the richness of the RRM, future versions could accommodate attrition and anniversary payments in accounting for costs. This would require further research on the interaction between enlistment incentives, IET completion, and first-term continuation.

[16] The RRM is designed to predict the outcome of resources allocated over a fiscal year. Since six months of pre–fiscal year advertising data are required given the nature of the advertising response function, the RRM cannot be validated on FY 2012.

- Fiscal year resourcing levels (including TV prospect advertising costs for six months prior to the start of the fiscal year)
- Monthly unemployment rates
- Monthly measure of recruiting difficulty
- Distribution of training seats across the fiscal year.

To conduct an in-sample validation of the RRM, we use the realized values for these inputs. The results are presented in Table 4.17. The model does very well for 2014, the year used for the underlying distribution of company-level and DEP characteristics, and 2015. It also does reasonably well in 2013 when the accession goal was approximately 12,000 greater than in 2014. It is important to recognize that these results are generated from the aggregation of the recruiting companies' predicted outputs based on recruiting resources, recruit eligibility policies, and recruiting environment. The model does not rely on a previous year's production level[17] and captures the productivity of resources in a structured way. In the next chapter, we demonstrate how the RRM can be used to consider the cost trade-offs of alternative resourcing or recruit eligibility plans, determine optimal resourcing policies for alternative recruiting goals, and determine differences in resourcing requirements under alternative recruiting conditions.

---

[17] The exception concerns the entry pool for the current year, which is an input to the RRM, or when the RRM is used for a multiple-year scenario, which uses the exit DEP for a given year as the entry pool for the following year.

Table 4.17
In-Sample Validation Test of the RRM

	FY 2013	FY 2014	FY 2015
Contracts	68,145	62,307	62,359
Accessions	69,085	57,101	59,177
Exit DEP	18,816	16,479	15,207
Contracts predicted	64,189	60,942	62,743
Accessions predicted	69,085	57,102	59,177
Exit DEP predicted	16,232	16,828	14,885
% of contracts	94	98	101
% of accessions	100	100	100
% of accessions + exit DEP	97	100	100

NOTE: The first three rows reflect realized values in FY 2013–2015. The second three rows reflect the predictions of the RRM. The final three rows reflect how close the predicted values were to the realized values. Accession goals will be close to 100 percent if sufficient contracts are produced within the fiscal year in a timely way to meet training seat vacancies. Since training seats cannot be overfilled, surplus production results in contracts having extended DEP lengths.

CHAPTER FIVE
Model Demonstration and Optimization

The RRM, discussed in detail in the last chapter, can be used to predict how a chosen set of recruiting resources, recruit eligibility policies, and the recruiting environment combine to produce accessions, an entry pool for the following year, and a resourcing cost. Military planners can use the RRM to determine whether the current resourcing plan is sufficient to achieve the Army's recruiting and quality goals. It is also possible to consider alternative combinations of resources, eligibility policies, and environments. This can assist military planners wanting to allocate resources in the most cost-efficient way, provide senior leaders with potential cost-eligibility trade-offs, or help leaders prepare for a potential change in the recruiting environment.

In this chapter, we introduce an optimization algorithm that is integrated with the RRM to provide a planning resource we refer to as the RRM tool. The algorithm determines the optimal allocation of resource levels and mix based on accession goals, entry pool goals for the next fiscal year, recruit eligibility policies, and resource costs. We begin by discussing use of the tool to predict production for a fixed resourcing plan under fixed or varying recruiting or eligibility conditions. This type of analysis can be used to help policymakers identify potential problems in meeting the Army's recruiting requirements under an existing plan and policy set. We then provide six examples of how the RRM tool can be used to inform policymakers about potential trade-offs or prepare for alternative environments. These examples include cost trade-offs based on

1. alternative recruiting environments
2. alternative resourcing strategies
3. alternative recruit eligibility policies
4. midyear goal or policy changes
5. five-year planning
6. alternative accession goals.

These examples demonstrate the versatility of the RRM. We conclude this chapter by discussing important conceptual details when using the RRM tool for planning purposes and potential extensions of the RRM tool that might further increase its versatility and applicability for military planners.

Optimization Algorithm

A key goal of this research is to determine an optimal resource mix for accomplishing recruiting targets. We define optimal as being the cost-minimizing bundle of resources that accomplishes the fiscal year accession and DEP goals conditional on a distribution of training seats across the fiscal year, an initial entry pool, starting resource levels (i.e., initial level of recruiters, prior six months of TV ad spending), enlistment quality objectives (e.g., HQ target, enlistment waivers, prior service accessions), and the recruiting environment.

The RRM produces estimates of fiscal year accessions, end-of-year DEP, and obligated costs.[1] Since these outcomes do not reflect a common unit, we must establish a criterion function that will weigh outcomes relative to one another and produce a single measure. We call this common, single measure the criterion value. Conceptually, the criterion value represents a way of comparing the cost difference between missing an accession goal by 100 recruits and spending an additional $1 million on recruiting resources. The criterion function will determine the point at which the optimization algorithm stops resourcing in par-

---

[1] We use the terminology "obligated" costs because it reflects payment commitments, such as bonuses, which may be paid out in future fiscal years.

ticularly difficult scenarios. Let $ADiff_t$ represent the difference between monthly accessions and the training seat goals for month t, $A1Diff_t$ represent the difference between monthly accessions and the training seat goals for month $t + 1$ as of month t, $DEPDiff_t$ represent the DEP shortfall in a given month, and $Cost_t$ represent the obligated costs from the resources allocated for that given month. Additionally, given the difference in units between dollars and accessions, we introduce weight vectors for accession-based differences that can vary based on whether the difference is positive or negative: W_A for the current month's accession difference, W_{A1} for month $t + 1$'s accession difference, and W_{DEP} for the DEP difference. The criterion function is specified as

$$\text{Criterion} = f\left(ADiff_t, W_A\right) + f\left(A1Diff_t, W_{A1}\right) +$$
$$f\left(DEPDiff_t, W_{DEP}\right) + Cost_t, \qquad (5.1)$$

where the function $f(\cdot)$ is represented by a piecewise function that gives different weights (i.e., $W_X = \{W_{X,1}, W_{X,2}\}$) to negative differences as compared to positive differences:

$$f\left(XDiff_t, W_X\right) = \begin{cases} W_{X,1} \cdot \left(XDiff_t\right)^2 & \text{if } XDiff_t < 0 \\ W_{X,2} \cdot \left(XDiff_t\right)^2 & \text{if } XDiff_t \geq 0, \end{cases}$$

and X is a placeholder for current accessions (A), next month's accessions (A1), and the current DEP.

The assumed weights of the criterion function are specified in Table 5.1. These relationships can be distilled mathematically into a more intuitive comparison. Missing a monthly accession goal by a shortfall of 100 training seats is equivalent to paying $15 million.[2] Put another way, the model would be willing to pay up to $15 million in additional resources to avoid missing by 100 training seats in that

---

[2] Following the formula just above, the difference is squared and then multiplied by the negative shortfall accession weight of 1,500 in Table 5.1.

month, or an average of $150,000 per contract. Willingness to pay diminishes the closer the model gets to the goals. The willingness to pay to avoid missing the first of the 100 training seats is $300,000, while the willingness to pay to avoid the last training seat missed is almost zero dollars. Since the model must be forward-looking to ensure that it achieves the target DEP size by the end of the fiscal year, the RRM keeps track of how many contracts are currently in the DEP relative to the target DEP size. The attained DEP size is based on the starting DEP size, the target end-of-year DEP size, and the distribution of training seats across the year. Missing the monthly DEP target by a shortfall of 1,000 contracts is equivalent to paying $30 million. Put another way, the model would be willing to pay up to $30 million in additional resources to avoid missing by 1,000 contracts in that month, or an average of $30,000 per contract. Again, the willingness to pay to reduce the shortfall diminishes as the model gets closer to achieving the objective. Specifically, it is willing to pay $60,000 to reduce the DEP shortfall for the first of the 1,000 contracts, while the willingness to pay to eliminate the last contract shortfall in the DEP is almost zero dollars. The parameterizations of the criterion function in Table 5.1 were calibrated to reflect differences in the size of monthly accession goals relative to the DEP size (e.g., common monthly accession goals range from 4,500 to 9,000 depending on the month of the year, whereas a preferred target DEP size would generally be at least 25 percent of annual accession goals, or about 17,000 in FY 2017) and to give strong priority to achieving accession goals (hence the substantially greater weight).[3] The choice of parameterizations also reflects extensive testing by the authors.

The optimization algorithm finds the most cost-effective combination of resources to achieve the monthly training seat goals and the end-of-year DEP size goal. The optimization algorithm works by calculating the marginal criterion value of each resource (e.g., the cost of one additional contract) and increases the resources with the lowest marginal criterion value. On the first iteration, enlistment incentives and TV ad spending begin at zero spending, and recruiters begin at a prespecified

---

[3]   Historically, Army planners have been willing to reduce the end-of-year DEP size in order to meet current accession goals.

Table 5.1
Criterion Function Weights

	Negative Differences (Shortfall)	Positive Differences (Surplus)
Current accessions	1,500	750
Next month's accessions (October–August)	30	7.5
Next month's accessions (September)	0	0
Exit DEP	30	7.5

NOTE: The values in the table represent the weights of Equation 5.1 as chosen by the authors.

starting point (this should match how many on-production recruiters the Army plans to have available at recruiting centers in the United States at the start of the fiscal year). The optimization algorithm tests an increase in enlistment incentive eligibility by 10 percentage points, an increase and a decrease in recruiters by 100, and an increase in TV ad spending by $1 million and $5 million in a month. To account for the nonlinearities associated with TV ad spending, we calculate the marginal criterion value for a small and a large change in TV advertising. The optimization continues to increase these resources in these increments until it cannot find a more cost-effective manner of increasing resources. At this point, all of the above increments are reduced to 10 percent of their original increment, and the search process begins again, until it cannot find a more cost-effective manner of increasing resources. Finally, all of the increments are reduced to 1 percent of their original increments, and the search process begins again, until it cannot find a more cost-effective manner of increasing resources. At this point, the optimization algorithm moves to the next month. For example, in the initial round, increases or decreases in recruiters are evaluated in increments of 100; in the second round, changes are evaluated in increments of 10; and in the final round, changes are evaluated in increments of 1.

The algorithm may not be able to find a more cost-effective manner of increasing resources, either because it achieves its goals or because it simply cannot produce enough contracts in a given month to achieve the month's accession and DEP targets. It is important to remember that when the RRM achieves its training seat goals for a given month (controlling for planned attrition), it extends the DEP of new contracts over future months (i.e., it builds the DEP size). Therefore, accession shortfalls typically occur when training seat goals are aggressive, and the model is unable to produce contracts that will access in a timely fashion. Examples of aggressive training seat goals include having a high training seat goal near the start of the fiscal year, when there is insufficient time to build the DEP, and having a prolonged period of high accession goals at the end of the year, where the model has to both fill immediate training seat vacancies and ensure a large DEP is sustained. In these cases, the optimization algorithm will likely choose to use quick-ship bonuses, with their shorter DEP lengths, to meet immediate training seat vacancies. In using the RRM tool, we assume the Army's objective is first to achieve the accession goal with its original monthly accession target. If the RRM tool is unable to efficiently allocate resources to achieve its goal given the existing distribution of monthly accession goals, then we raise the accession target to allow accessions to be produced in other months rather than stating that the Army is unable to achieve its annual accession goal. This process is repeated manually in small increments until at least 99.5 percent of the accession goal is achieved or further increases yield no appreciable gains.

Given the nature of our estimated TV advertising response function, where advertising in the past may influence current production, the optimization algorithm allows the model to increase TV advertising in previous months within the fiscal year. For example, when determining the optimal resourcing in November, the model will consider increasing October's TV ad spending. (It will not consider pre–fiscal year spending, as that is assumed to be fixed.) Likewise, in September, it will look retrospectively across the entire fiscal year. If the algorithm does consider increasing a past month's ad spending to meet the current month's goals, it will account for the additional marginal cost incurred in the past period as part of its current cost when making the decision.[4]

---

[4]   This only applies during the monthly optimization process. When numbers are reported, the cost is allocated to the month when TV ad money is spent.

Allowing retrospective TV ad spending is critical to efficient planning and can help the algorithm appropriately resource training seat targets in future months.

Additionally, we impose a few constraints on the optimization algorithm. First, based on our analysis of historical records, the number of recruiters is constrained to not increase by more than 1.6 percent in a month or to decrease by more than 1.0 percent in a month. Annually, this amounts to a maximum increase of 21 percent or a maximum decrease of 11 percent, which closely reflects the sharpest annual on-production RA recruiter growth and shrinkage rates observed in FY 2005 and FY 2012, respectively. These "throttles" for recruiter growth and shrinkage are intended to reflect operational limitations on changing the size of the recruiter workforce. Growing the number of recruiters in the short term can be accomplished through assignment extensions, and over the longer term, it can also be accomplished by identifying an increased number of qualified noncommissioned officers (NCO) for training and transfer to a new recruiting assignment. Drawing down the recruiter workforce in the short run generally requires waiting for the expiration of the recruiter's assignment, which creates a natural throttle on decreasing the size of the recruiter workforce. Over the longer term, reduction can also be accomplished by identifying a decreased number of qualified NCOs for training and transfer to a new recruiting assignment. Also, we limit enlistment incentives for non-HQ to be no greater than enlistment incentives for HQ contracts. This is meant to reflect how enlistment incentives are typically offered: at higher rates (both level and eligibility) to HQ contracts. Finally, the optimization algorithm sets bounds on ad spending, bonus levels, and bonus eligibility. Namely, ad spending cannot exceed $40 million in any month, eligibility cannot exceed 90 percent for enlistment incentives, and bonus levels cannot exceed $40,000.[5]

---

[5] These bounds are chosen based on previously observed maximums (e.g., as in the case of bonus eligibility), technical maximums (i.e., bonuses cannot exceed $40,000 for enlistment incentives), or levels above which the productivity is extremely small (i.e., $40 million is well above TV prospect advertising's saturation point).

Finally, the optimization algorithm does not currently allow optimization over enlistment bonus levels. Given the nature of our principal component model for bonuses, increasing bonus levels at low levels of contract production would result in an artificial increase in contract production for zero cost. In an optimization setting, this may lead to spurious results. Consequently, we only permit optimization over bonus eligibility and require a specified bonus level for each bonus type.

The optimization algorithm loops over each month in the fiscal year. After it reaches the final month, the optimization algorithm is repeated a second time, starting with the final level of TV ad spending, and optimizing over all resources again. This last step is intended to ensure that changes in TV advertising in earlier months of the fiscal year do not result in the inappropriate overuse of enlistment incentives or recruiters. As an example, consider the following scenario. Suppose enlistment incentives were used in October with zero ad spending. However, in December, the algorithm determines that it is optimal to use TV ad spending in October to meet its goals for December. In this case, October will now result in more contracts produced, potentially making it unnecessary to offer enlistment incentives (or potentially reducing their need).

In developing this optimization algorithm, we considered several alternative optimization algorithms. The alternative optimization algorithms included both derivative and nonderivative methods of optimizing. However, because of the nonlinearities of the contract production function and the complex interrelationship among the elements of the RRM, we found that these alternatives typically resulted in suboptimal resource allocation. The optimization algorithm developed in this chapter reflects the underlying design of the RRM and captures the complex interrelationships that are part of the Army recruiting effort.

The final result of the optimization algorithm is an efficient allocation of resources, contracts, and accessions across the fiscal year. In the next sections, we provide several examples of using the RRM in practice. Unless otherwise specified, we use the optimization algorithm. The optimization algorithm as presented here is referred to as version 1.0, in anticipation that future updates to the RRM tool after this report will reflect improvements in this process. The version of the RRM tool and its algorithm are reported in the output produced by the RRM tool in order to facilitate comparisons among users.

Analyzing Current Resourcing and Eligibility Plans

The RRM can consider an existing recruiting resource and recruit eligibility plan for a fiscal year and, without optimizing resources, predict whether the plan is capable of achieving the accession and end-of-year DEP goals. For example, consider a hypothetical resourcing and eligibility plan:

- Resources:
    - MOS bonuses: 43 percent bonus eligibility for HQ contracts, with a $12,000 average bonus. No eligibility for non-HQ contracts. This corresponds to levels and eligibility from October to December 2016.
    - Quick-ship bonuses: 35 percent bonus eligibility for HQ contracts, with a $15,000 average bonus. No eligibility for non-HQ contracts. This corresponds to levels and eligibility from October to December 2016.
    - TV prospect advertising: $3 million per month, including the six months prior to the fiscal year. Corresponds to a low level of TV prospect advertising.
    - Recruiters: 8,100 on-production recruiters per month. This corresponds to the level as of October 2016.

- Recruit eligibility:
    - HQ percentage: 55 percent with traditional high school diploma and scoring in the top half of the AFQT score distribution. This corresponds to the HQ percentage in FY 2016.
    - Enlistment waivers: 12 percent with waivers. This corresponds to the FY 2012–2016 average. The FY 2016 waiver rate was 12.6 percent.
    - Prior service accessions: 3,000. This corresponds to the approximate number of prior service in FY 2016.

- Recruiting environment:
  - Civilian unemployment rate: 4.8 percent. This corresponds to the rate as of October 2016.
  - Contracts in DEP at start of FY 2017: 16,522.
  - Training seat distribution: Monthly training seats based on original FY 2017 ODCS G-1 mission letter distribution, proportionately scaled up to reflect an annual accession goal of 68,500.

The RRM predicts that this combination of resources, eligibility policies, and environment would result in 62,867 accessions in FY 2017 and an entry pool for the following year of approximately 13,380. The total cost is estimated at $1.3 billion, divided 73 percent, 3 percent, and 24 percent among recruiters ($956 million), TV prospect advertising ($36 million), and enlistment incentives ($312 million).[6] These results suggest that this resourcing plan would have been sufficient to meet the original FY 2017 accession goal of 62,500, but would have been insufficient to meet the revised FY 2017 accession goal of 68,500.

The plan evaluated above did not make use of the RRM's optimization algorithm. In the next six examples, we demonstrate how the RRM tool can be used strategically to inform policymakers about potential trade-offs or to prepare for alternative environments.

---

[6]   As discussed earlier, by design, the costs estimated by the RRM tool are intended to allow decisionmakers to examine strategic choices in recruiting resourcing and enlistment eligibility policies and differ from the exact amounts that would need to be budgeted for a given fiscal year. For example, among the costs included, the estimated bonus cost is conservative, because, due to attrition, the eventual payout for bonuses will be less than the amount indicated, since it is paid upon completing IET and, for bonuses exceeding $10,000, the amount in excess of $10,000 is paid out in equal installments on annual anniversaries of accession across the first term. A consequence of this is that when the RRM optimizes across resources, it will overestimate the cost of expanding bonus eligibility relative to the other resources at the margin. The recruiter cost supplied by HQDA is based on compensation rather than recruiting operations. TV prospect advertising cost represents the cost of media buys and, thus, is a subset of all marketing costs. Last, some costs, such as those related to the Military Entrance Processing Command, are not included in the RRM tool. As noted, the tool can be adapted for budgeting purposes; we expect to carry out the budget adaptation in future work.

Alternative Recruiting Environments

An important part of resource planning is considering potential contingencies. In this section, we consider how alternative recruiting environments would alter optimal resource planning for FY 2018 based on the observed environment as of the start of FY 2017. We consider a hypothetical example where the accession goal for 2018 is 75,000 and the target entry pool for FY 2019 is 20,000. We assume the entry pool for FY 2018 is only 12,500. Recruit eligibility characteristics are assumed to be a target HQ accession goal of 57 percent, 12 percent enlistment waivers, and 3,000 prior service accessions. The training seat distribution is assumed to follow the distribution of seats in the October 2016 ODCS G-1 mission letter, with training seats concentrated in January and July–September.[7] The starting number of on-production recruiters at centers is assumed to be 8,800, and TV prospect ad spending in the last six months of the fiscal year ranges from $5.6 to $8 million in April to July, with near-zero spending in August and September. These characteristics represent our baseline scenario and will be used as a common reference point throughout this chapter.

For this example, we consider two scenarios reflecting alternative, potential recruiting environments. The first scenario assumes that the economic environment begins to revert to the long-run mean (by the end of FY 2022) at the beginning of FY 2017, with unemployment rising from 4.8 percent, where it was at the beginning of FY 2017, to 5.2 percent on average over FY 2018. Likewise, the other economic inputs in Wenger et al.'s (forthcoming) Recruiting Difficulty Index model, including housing starts and the University of Michigan Consumer Sentiment Index, also move toward their long-run means over this time period. We assume the noneconomic variables in the Recruiting Difficulty Index model are unchanged over this period (e.g., adverse events measure). The second scenario assumes that the recruiting environment is where it was at the beginning of FY 2017, with unemployment holding constant at 4.8 percent through FY 2018. Variation in the recruiting environment affects the RRM through two vehicles: unemployment

---

[7]   The specific training seat distribution is provided in Figure 5.3.

rate and national recruiting difficulty. Changes in the unemployment rate filter down to the company level by assuming a change in the local level unemployment rate that is proportional to the national trend. The recruiting environment predictions, based on Wenger et al.'s (forthcoming) Recruiting Difficulty Index, are in the form of the 12-month moving averages of GA contract mission attainment rates.

Table 5.2 demonstrates that the recruiting objective is feasible if all resources are used; however, the cost and resource usage varies between the two scenarios. Under the more difficult recruiting environment (Scenario 2), the model predicts an additional $238 million is required (relative to Scenario 1). All resources are increased to meet the objective, but 75 percent ($178 million) of the additional resources are allocated to bonuses. The model finds heavy use of quick-ship bonuses from February to April is required in order to meet a significant May accession goal. Figure 5.1 reveals that even with heavier bonus usage, Scenario 2 requires some training seats to be pushed beyond May, increasing the numbers from June to September in order to meet the accession goal.[8] Prior to May, the distribution of training seats is such that even with a more difficult recruiting environment, the RRM predicts the Army would be able to achieve its first- and second-quarter accession targets.

Ultimately, achieving the accession requirement in the more difficult recruiting environment comes at the sacrifice of DEP for the next fiscal year—in Scenario 2 the DEP for next year is almost 3,000 short (only 96.9 percent of the accession goal plus exit DEP goal of 95,000 was achieved). It is important to be careful in interpreting these results: one should not automatically interpret the missed DEP goal as an indicator that it is not possible for both the accession and DEP goals to be achieved under the more difficult Scenario 2. That is because we have assumed a fixed training seat distribution that permits training seats to be pushed later in the fiscal year only when they are missed. A forward-looking planner using the RRM should consider a variety of training seat distributions or, alternatively, a higher accession or DEP

---

[8]   There are limitations on reallocating training seats and increasing the number of trainees per class.

Table 5.2
Cost Comparison for Alternative Recruiting Environments

Recruit Characteristics and Recruiting Resources	Scenario 1: FY 2018 Recruiting Environment	Scenario 2: FY 2018 Recruiting Environment
Percentage of HQ accessions target	57	57
Percentage of waivers	12	12
Prior service target	3,000	3,000
Average annual unemployment rate	5.2	4.8
Recruiters (average across FY)	9,196	9,325
Recruiter costs ($M)	1,085	1,100
TV prospect ad costs ($M)	349	394
Bonus costs ($M)	177	355
Total costs ($M)	1,611	1,849
Percentage of accession goal achieved	99.6	99.6
Percentage of accession + exit DEP goal achieved	99.0	96.9

NOTE: The optimal resource allocations are determined by the RRM, which used the RRM optimization algorithm version 1.0. Costs are reported in millions of dollars. The RRM optimizes monthly resource obligations to achieve an accession goal of 75,000 and an end-of-year DEP goal of 20,000. Key assumptions include monthly training seats based on original FY 2017 ODCS G-1 mission letter distribution; 8,800 recruiters at start of fiscal year; $8, $5.7, $8.7, $7.1, $0.2, and $0.2 million in monthly ad spending prior to start of fiscal year (April–September, respectively); 12,500 entry DEP; recruiting environment varies, as described in text.

goal that will allow overproduction during the year and change the resourcing balance. These outcomes may result in lower costs, greater DEP production, or both. We will expand on important conceptual details when using the RRM tool for planning purposes at the end of this chapter.

Figure 5.1
Predicted Monthly Accession Achievement Under Alternative Recruiting Environments

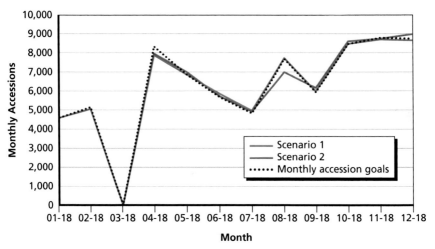

NOTE: See note below Table 5.2.
RAND *RR2364A-5.1*

Alternative Resourcing Strategies

A key strength of the RRM when combined with the optimization algorithm described in this chapter is its ability to determine the cost-efficient allocation of resources. In this section, we consider an incentive-centric strategy. Incentives are considered to be a fast-acting resource that can be deployed when objectives change or when difficult recruiting conditions arise. In these cases, other resources often cannot be changed quickly enough to meet training seat objectives. However, that responsiveness comes at a cost, which is what we illustrate here. In this example, we consider a scenario where a planner follows an incentive-centric strategy from the beginning of the fiscal year. We define an incentive-centric strategy as one where the optimization algorithm attempts to achieve the recruiting objectives by changing only enlistment incentives (i.e., it fixes recruiters at their starting level and TV prospect ad spending at zero). After this initial attempt, it does a second run through the optimization algorithm allowing all resources to increase (and decrease in the case of recruiters), but it will not decrease bonuses. Using the same example as in the last section with a constant recruiting environment, Table 5.3 presents a comparison between a full-optimization strategy (allowing all three resources to be used) and the incentive-centric strategy just outlined. The result is a $354 million difference to accomplish the fiscal year accession goals. The cost difference is driven by an additional $419 million being spent on bonuses, $37 million less spent on TV advertising, and $27 million less spent on recruiters.

The dynamics of how the accession goals are achieved, despite a sharp increase in bonus spending, are quite informative. In Figure 5.2, we overlay the monthly accession achievement produced by the RRM and the monthly recruiter numbers. At an accession target of 75,000, the incentive-centric scenario was unable to use resources in an efficient way to meet the monthly accession targets, particularly at the end of the fiscal year. In order to accomplish 75,000 accessions during the fiscal year, we increased the accession target to 78,000, which allowed greater production earlier in the first half of the fiscal year.

This example highlights the importance of appropriate resource allocation when sufficient planning time is available. The initial focus on enlistment incentives allows the incentive-centric strategy to achieve the accessions through July; however, in doing so, not only is the policy more expensive, but it also places the recruiting enterprise at a disadvantage heading into the summer months, as the recruiting force is too small to accomplish the summer recruiting objectives. By the summer months, recruiters cannot be increased sufficiently to make up the difference. Consequently, the model underproduces in the last couple of months of the fiscal year, and bonuses are insufficient to make up the difference.

Alternative Recruit Eligibility Policies

The cost of the last contract produced when the accession goal is 75,000 is far greater than the cost of the last contract produced when the acces-

Table 5.3
Cost Comparison of Alternative Resource Strategies

Recruit Characteristics and Recruiting Resources	Full Optimization Strategy	Incentive-Centric Strategy
Percentage of HQ accessions target	57	57
Percentage of waivers	12	12
Prior service target	3,000	3,000
Average annual unemployment rate	4.8	4.8
Recruiters (average across FY)	9,325	9,093
Recruiter costs ($M)	1,100	1,073
TV prospect ad costs ($M)	394	357
Bonus costs ($M)	355	774
Total costs ($M)	1,849	2,203
Percentage of accession goal achieved	99.6	99.8
Percentage of accession + exit DEP goal achieved	96.9	98.3

NOTE: The optimal resource allocations are determined by the RRM, which used the RRM optimization algorithm version 1.0. Costs are reported in millions of dollars. The RRM optimizes monthly resource obligations to achieve an accession goal of 75,000 and an end-of-year DEP goal of 20,000. Key assumptions include monthly training seats based on original FY 2017 ODCS G-1 mission letter distribution; 8,800 recruiters at FY start; $8, $5.7, $8.7, $7.1, $0.2, and $0.2 million in monthly ad spending prior to start of fiscal year (April–September, respectively); 12,500 entry DEP; the recruiting environment reflects economic conditions remaining constant. In the incentive-centric scenario, bonuses are used first to accomplish fiscal year objectives and, if there is an accession shortfall, the RRM uses other resources to make up the difference. In the incentive-centric scenario, the accession goal used in the RRM was set to 78,000 to allow sufficient accessions to achieve at least 99.5 percent of the 75,000 accession goal.

Figure 5.2
Monthly Accessions and Recruiters Under Alternative Resourcing Plans

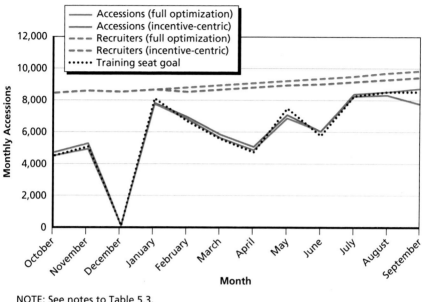

NOTE: See notes to Table 5.3.
RAND RR2364A-5.2

sion goal is only 60,000. Likewise, the cost of the last contract produced in difficult recruiting conditions is far greater than the last contract produced in an easy recruiting environment. To ensure that the Army reaches its accession goals, expanding recruit eligibility represents an alternative that lowers immediate costs and can help achieve particularly onerous recruiting objectives. The RRM can be used to consider the cost trade-offs of changing recruit eligibility requirements. A separate model, known as the Recruit Selection Tool (see Orvis et al., forthcoming), can be used in conjunction with the RRM tool to consider the accession and first-term cost trade-offs of expanding eligibility. This includes changes in recruiting requirements and costs due to changes in attrition rates, changes in costs related to training performance and throughput, and, as appropriate, the greater Regular Military Compensation costs of prior service recruits, among other outcomes.

Before considering an example illustrating the RRM-related cost trade-offs of alternative recruit eligibility policies, it is important to remember how eligibility enters into the RRM. For quality targets, the RRM has separate contract production functions for HQ and for overall RA contracts. Lowering the target HQ rate allows more non-HQ to be produced (up to the goal or to the ceiling that the RA production function can produce for RA contracts). For waivers, the RRM amplifies overall contract production by the ratio of the target waiver rate to the historical waiver rate during the period when the contract production functions were estimated. Finally, for prior service, the RRM distributes additional prior service contracts evenly across the year. The model assumes that the additional contracts produced through waivers and prior service allotments occur at the target HQ rate. Additionally, since changes in the recruiting environment and resources directly affect contract production, they alter the number of recruits gained through HQ and waiver goal changes in recruit eligibility policies, and vice versa. These assumptions regarding how eligibility enters the RRM mean that this model assumes that eligibility criteria are limited by the Army's demand. Consequently, an expansion in eligibility opens the doors to individuals who would have enlisted, all else equal. In extreme cases this assumption may not hold true, leading to underestimating actual recruiting costs, if the resources required to recruit these additional individuals at the margin exceed those used in the RRM. It is important that a user of the RRM tool remember these assumptions when interpreting the model's output.

In Table 5.4 we consider three separate expansions of recruit eligibility policy for our baseline accession goal of 75,000 with 57 percent HQ target, 12 percent waivers, and 3,000 prior service accessions. In each case, we consider an expansion of 3 percentage points relative to the accession goal:

1. Lower HQ target to 54 percent
2. Increase waivers to 15 percent
3. Increase prior service accessions to 5,250 (e.g., achieve an additional 3 percent of the accession goal through prior service accessions).

Accession achievement is similar across the scenarios, but reductions in costs range from $113 million for expanded waivers to $143 million for decreasing the HQ target. The last column in Table 5.4 considers changes in all three criteria. The reduction in costs for changing all three criteria is $429 million, which is $47 million less than the cumulative reductions of each eligibility lever applied individually. This suggests that the eligibility policies are interrelated, but to a relatively limited degree.

The results in Table 5.4 indicate that expanding eligibility can significantly reduce resource costs during the fiscal year. As a result, recruit eligibility represents an important policy lever that Army planners should consider when developing resourcing plans.

Midyear Policy Changes

Sudden changes in recruiting requirements or the environment may force a correction to earlier resourcing plans. The optimization algorithm can be adjusted to optimize over shorter periods within the fiscal year. For example, in FY 2017 following the passage of the 2017 National Defense Authorization Act, the Army increased the fiscal year accession requirement from 62,500 to 68,500. This change occurred in January, the start of the second quarter of FY 2017. Consequently, resources needed to be increased and reallocated to meet this new, higher accession goal.

The RRM allows for this type of midyear analysis. In Table 5.3, we demonstrated that an incentive-centric resourcing plan was costly. In Table 5.5, we reproduce this result in the first column for reference. In the next column, we consider an alternative where the RRM is permitted to efficiently allocate resources starting at the beginning of the fourth quarter. Costs are lower by $143 million and the accession target is still achieved, because even a little time allows for the resourcing plan to efficiently reallocate resources. Then, in the next two columns we consider an earlier start date at the beginning of the third and second quarters, respectively. As optimal resourcing is started sooner, overall resourcing costs are substantively reduced. The last column reproduces

Table 5.4
Cost Comparison of Alternative Recruit Eligibility Policies

Recruit Characteristics and Recruiting Resources	Baseline	Scenario 1: Lower HQ Target	Scenario 2: Increase Waivers	Scenario 3: Greater Prior Service	Expanded Eligibility on All Dimensions
Percentage of HQ accessions target	57	54	57	57	54.0
Percentage of waivers	12	12	15	12	15
Prior service target	3,000	3,000	3,000	5,250	5,250
Average annual unemployment rate	4.8	4.8	4.8	4.8	4.8
Recruiters (average across FY)	9,325	9,108	9,108	9,099	8,466
Recruiter costs ($M)	1,100	1,075	1,075	1,074	999
TV prospect ad costs ($M)	394	380	378	392	354
Bonus costs ($M)	355	251	284	259	67
Total costs ($M)	1,849	1,706	1,736	1,724	1,420
Percentage of accession goal achieved	99.6	100.4	99.6	99.6	99.9
Percentage of accession + exit DEP goal achieved	96.9	99.1	98.0	98.1	99.2

NOTE: The optimal resource allocations are determined by the RRM, which used the RRM optimization algorithm version 1.0. Costs are reported in millions of dollars. The RRM optimizes monthly resource obligations to achieve an accession goal of 75,000 and an end-of-year DEP goal of 20,000. Key assumptions include monthly training seats based on original FY 2017 ODCS G-1 mission letter distribution; 8,800 recruiters at start of fiscal year; $8, $5.7, $8.7, $7.1, $0.2, and $0.2 million in monthly ad spending prior to start of fiscal year (April–September, respectively); 12,500 entry DEP; the recruiting environment reflects economic conditions remaining constant. In Scenario 1, the accession goal used in the RRM was set to 75,500 to allow sufficient accessions to achieve at least 99.5 percent of the 75,000 accession goal.

the optimal resourcing plan if it were started in the first quarter, which is simply the optimal resourcing plan from Table 5.2.

Table 5.5 demonstrates cost savings from adjusting resources sooner rather than later. The optimization algorithm is also flexible enough to consider alternative timing for when resources can be changed. A common example is that of advertising. The Army advertising budget corresponds to the calendar year, as opposed to the fiscal year. If advertising dollars for a calendar year are spent before the October start of the next fiscal year, then the advertising budget may not be able to be changed for the first quarter of the next fiscal year. The optimization algorithm for the RRM is designed to allow the military planner flexibility in choosing which resources can be optimized and when resources can be changed.

Five-Year Planning

In addition to next fiscal year planning and midyear adjustments, Army planners are routinely called on to make resource planning assumptions for a five-year period ending up to seven years in the future. This type of planning requires substantial assumptions regarding accession goals and the recruiting environment. As demonstrated above, both the goals and the environment can have a dramatic effect on cost. The RRM tool has been developed with this long-term planning in mind. It can take national-level outputs from one year and use them as inputs for the next year. The required inputs for a five-year resourcing assessment include target accession goals for each fiscal year and the DEP goal for the next fiscal year; recruit eligibility targets for each fiscal year; recruiting environment assumptions for all 60 months; monthly distribution of training seats; and starting levels of resources (e.g., recruiters and prior six months of TV prospect advertising). Also, this assessment, along with all assessments using the RRM tool, makes the assumption that the geographical distribution of recruiters, unemployment, missioning, population, and contract productivity remain as they were in FY 2014. As a demonstration of the five-year planning capability, we consider an example using our baseline scenario of a 75,000 accession goal in 2018

Table 5.5
Cost Comparison of Midyear Policy Changes

Recruit Characteristics and Recruiting Resources	Incentive-Centric Resourcing Plan	Resources Are Optimally Allocated Starting in 4th Quarter	Resources Are Optimally Allocated Starting in 3rd Quarter	Resources Are Optimally Allocated Starting in 2nd Quarter	Resources Are Optimally Allocated Starting in 1st Quarter
Percentage of HQ accessions target	57	57	57	57	57
Percentage of waivers	12	12	12	12	12
Prior service target	3,000	3,000	3,000	3,000	3,000
Average annual unemployment rate	4.8	4.8	4.8	4.8	4.8
Recruiters (average across FY)	9,093	9,103	9,127	9,318	9,325
Recruiter costs ($M)	1,073	1,074	1,077	1,100	1,100
TV prospect ad costs ($M)	357	353	357	367	394
Bonus costs ($M)	774	633	529	429	355
Total costs ($M)	2,203	2,060	1,963	1,896	1,849
Percentage of accession goal achieved	99.8	99.6	100.5	100.0	99.6
Percentage of accession + exit DEP goal achieved	98.3	97.6	97.5	97.5	96.9

NOTE: The optimal resource allocations are determined by the RRM, which used the RRM optimization algorithm version 1.0. Costs are reported in millions of dollars. The RRM optimizes monthly resource obligations to achieve an accession goal of 75,000 and an end-of-year DEP goal of 20,000. Key assumptions include monthly training seats based on original FY 2017 ODCS G1 mission letter distribution; 8,800 recruiters at start of fiscal year; $8, $5.7, $8.7, $7.1, $0.2, and $0.2 million in monthly ad spending prior to start of fiscal year (April–September, respectively); 12,500 entry DEP; the recruiting environment reflects economic conditions remaining constant. In the third-quarter scenario, the accession goal used in the RRM was set to 75,500 to allow sufficient accessions to achieve at least 99.5 percent of the 75,000 accession goal.

that plans to grow the force by increasing accession goals to 80,000 in FY 2019, and to 82,000 from FY 2020 to FY 2022. In each case, we set the end-of-year DEP target to 25 percent of the next year's accession goal. We maintain the constant recruiting environment assumption with continuing low unemployment and a persistent recruiting difficulty index based on Wenger et al.'s (forthcoming) model. Table 5.6 presents the results. Starting in FY 2019, each year takes the past year's end-of-year recruiter levels, DEP, and advertising as a starting point for its optimization. The model finds that the recruiting objectives are generally achievable despite the persistently difficult recruiting environment. The RRM tool predicts that to grow the accessions and the DEP over the first two years of this example, the recruiting force will need to be gradually increased over this time period, TV prospect advertising will need to be increased and maintained at high levels, and bonuses will need to be used heavily in conjunction with the other resources. Over the next three years, given an established and substantial entry pool, bonuses are predicted to be used less heavily, but all resources are used to produce the higher accession goals. Growth in the end-of-year DEP and the recruiting force over the first three years establishes a foundation with which to meet the sustained high level of recruiting demand for the last two years of the planning horizon. Consequently, the average cost per accession is continually falling over this period.

The five-year planning results in Table 5.6 using the RRM tool optimize results within year and distribute the entry pool for each year based on the methods described in Chapter Four. It is possible that more cost-efficient five-year planning outcomes could be achieved if the model were optimized over all five years.[9] It is important to remember that reported costs correspond to the resources committed to during the fiscal year, which may differ from how resources are accounted for in Army budgeting. This is particularly important for enlistment incentives, which are paid in anniversary payments over the recruit's first term of service for bonuses exceeding $10,000. This means that the cost of these bonuses, for Army budget purposes, can be distributed across

---

[9] While this is a potential extension of the optimization algorithm, it would substantially increase computational time from hours to days.

Table 5.6
Five-Year Planning Horizon for Recruiting Resources

Recruit Characteristics and Recruiting Resources	FY 2018	FY 2019	FY 2020	FY 2021	FY 2022
Accession goal	75,000	80,000	82,000	82,000	82,000
End-of-year DEP goal	20,000	20,500	20,500	20,500	20,500
Percentage of HQ accessions target	57.0	57.0	57.0	57.0	57.0
Percentage of waivers	12	12	12	12	12
Prior service target	3,000	3,000	3,000	3,000	3,000
Average annual unemployment rate	4.8	4.8	4.8	4.8	4.8
Recruiters (average across FY)	9,325	10,460	11,718	12,213	12,040
Recruiter costs ($M)	1,100	1,234	1,383	1,441	1,421
TV prospect ad costs ($M)	394	403	401	389	369
Bonus costs ($M)	355	360	320	150	136
Total costs ($M)	1,849	1,997	2,103	1,980	1,926
Average cost per accession	24,754	25,014	25,704	24,239	23,559
Percentage of accession goal achieved	99.6	99.8	99.8	99.6	99.7
Percentage of accession + exit DEP goal achieved	96.9	97.1	98.5	98.8	98.9

NOTE: The optimal resource allocations are determined by the Recruiting Resource Model, which used the RRM optimization algorithm version 1.0. Costs are reported in millions of dollars. The RRM optimizes monthly resource obligations to achieve listed accession and end-of-year DEP goals. Key assumptions include monthly training seats based on original FY 2017 ODCS G-1 mission letter distribution; 8,800 recruiters at start of fiscal year; $8, $5.7, $8.7, $7.1, $0.2, and $0.2 million in monthly ad spending prior to start of fiscal year (April–September, respectively); 12,500 entry DEP; the recruiting environment reflects economic conditions remaining constant. In FY 2019 and FY 2020 scenarios, the accession goal used in the RRM was set to 80,500 and 82,500, respectively, to allow sufficient accessions to achieve at least 99.5 percent of each fiscal year accession goal.

multiple fiscal years and can be reduced by attrition. We will expand on important conceptual details when using the RRM tool for planning purposes at the end of this chapter.

Alternative Accession Goals

Our examples of the RRM tool's capabilities have thus far focused on a 75,000 accession goal (the average of the post-drawdown era, FY 1994–2010), but this goal is high relative to post–FY 2010 accession goals, which have ranged from 57,000 to 69,000. In this example, we consider our baseline scenario, but with the lower accession goals of 68,500 and 60,000. In Table 5.7, as accession goals are decreased, total costs fall by $301 million and $693 million relative to our baseline scenario. The allocation of resources decreases markedly, with the recruiter force optimally decreasing in size as the accession goals decline, and TV prospect advertising and bonuses decreasing markedly. Bonus costs decrease the quickest as accession goals fall. This is due to the high initial starting level of recruiters (8,800) and the fact that, with sufficient planning time, enlistment incentives can be avoided by resourcing appropriately in the first two quarters of the fiscal year, in order to build contracts to meet high fourth-quarter accession goals.

Summary

The RRM produces monthly accessions and end-of-year DEP size for a specified level of recruiting resources, enlistment eligibility policies, the recruiting environment, and the training seat distribution. When combined with an optimization algorithm, the RRM can be used by Army planners to compare costs and mission achievement across a range of alternative environmental, resource, eligibility, training seat, and timing assumptions. We refer to this resource as the RRM tool. This chapter has highlighted many examples of how the RRM tool can be used. It represents a versatile tool for considering trade-offs across the recruiting enterprise. In doing so, it can provide resourcing alternatives that

Table 5.7
Cost Comparison of Alternative Accession Goals

Recruit Characteristics and Recruiting Resources	Baseline	Mid-Level Accession Goal	Low-Level Accession Goal
Accession goal	75,000	68,500	60,000
End-of-year DEP goal	20,000	20,000	20,000
Percentage of HQ accessions target	57.0	57.0	57.0
Percentage of waivers	12	12	12
Prior service target	3,000	3,000	3,000
Average annual unemployment rate	4.8	4.8	4.8
Recruiters (average across FY)	9,325	8,856	8,300
Recruiter costs ($M)	1,100	1,045	979
TV prospect ad costs ($M)	394	375	177
Bonus costs ($M)	355	128	0
Total costs ($M)	1,849	1,549	1,156
Percentage of accession goal achieved	99.6	99.9	100.0
Percentage of accession + exit DEP goal achieved	96.9	98.8	99.6

NOTE: The optimal resource allocations are determined by the RRM, which used the RRM optimization algorithm version 1.0. Costs are reported in millions of dollars. The RRM optimizes monthly resource obligations to achieve listed accession and end-of-year DEP goals. Key assumptions include monthly training seats based on original FY 2017 ODCS G-1 mission letter distribution; 8,800 recruiters at start of fiscal year; $8, $5.7, $8.7, $7.1, $0.2, and $0.2 million in monthly ad spending prior to start of fiscal year (April–September, respectively); 12,500 entry DEP; the recruiting environment reflects economic conditions remaining constant.

can achieve accession goals and potentially save hundreds of millions of resourcing dollars.

It is important for military planners to remember that the key outcomes produced by the RRM, namely, accessions and costs, reflect the underlying assumptions of the RRM tool. Accession achievement may vary from observed outcomes because the realized monthly resourcing levels, eligibility, environment, and training seat distribution differ from the assumptions made. For example, the RRM does not allow for monthly training seat vacancies to be overfilled unless previous months' vacancies have not been filled. The RRM reflects a contract production function estimated on FY 2012–2015 data, and assumes the geographical distribution of recruiting companies, recruiters, advertising viewership, population, missioning, and DEP attrition rates from FY 2014. As time passes, these distributions could change, potentially causing the predicted results to deviate more from the observed results. Additionally, changes in eligibility conditions generally assume that eligibility policy constrains demand. At very expanded levels of eligibility, it is possible that these assumptions are not valid and that further eligibility expansion exhibits diminishing marginal productivity. The RRM tool assumes that all recruiting resources are flexible, which may not be true because of separate allocations in the Army's budget or required lead time to change resourcing. There may also be reasons for using recruiting resources that are not captured by the RRM tool, such as using enlistment incentives for directing recruits into specific MOSs, using TV advertising to build the Army brand, and retaining a high level of recruiters to ensure against future difficult recruiting environments. As discussed, the RRM tool minimizes the cost of the resources needed to achieve a specific month's training seat goals, and this annual obligated cost is what is reflected in our bottom-line numbers throughout this chapter. The cost used for this optimization may differ from the cost required for Army budgeting purposes. For example, bonus costs assume bonuses are paid to those who access (which accounts for DEP attrition), but, as discussed earlier, large bonuses are actually paid over the enlistee's first term, which means bonus costs may be lower due to first-term attrition. Another example is that the RRM does not consider the cost of non–TV prospect advertising, which includes TV advertising aimed at influencers, advertising through other media (e.g., social media, internet), or the fixed costs of marketing contracts.

In light of the assumptions above, we encourage users of the RRM tool to consider the following checks when conducting an analysis with the tool. First, ensure that assumptions are consistent when comparing across alternative scenarios—the tool outputs both starting assumptions and the optimal allocation of resources for comparative purposes. Second, when considering high accession goals, like the baseline scenario used in this chapter, consider testing slightly higher accession and DEP goals before concluding that a specific accession goal is unachievable.[10] For reasons laid out in the discussion of the optimization algorithm, the algorithm may stop resourcing an objective because it considers the resources required to achieve the last 100 or so training seats in a month as being too expensive. Raising accession goals reflects that the Army will overfill training seat vacancies, and will generally result in exceeding the annual accession goal by a small margin. Third, the RRM tool is most effective when comparing trade-offs for planning purposes, so we encourage users to focus on the differences in relative costs rather than the exact cost levels. Since the costs for determining optimal resourcing may differ from how the Army allocates costs for budgeting, it is important to establish a baseline level from which to compare the results when considering the cost implications of changes in resourcing and eligibility policy strategies.

The caveats described above suggest some important potential extensions for the RRM tool. First, while the model is currently focused on informing the recruiting enterprise, its output can be adapted to inform both budget and training planning. As the model tracks accession timing and characteristics, it can be adapted to allocate costs and training seats commensurate with what is required for Army planning purposes. Second, the model could be adapted to incorporate USAR accessions. Third, the model could be adapted to examine the role of internet and social media advertising (this project is currently under way). Finally, the model could be adapted to examine potential options for reallocating resources across recruiting companies.

While the assumptions and caveats associated with the model may seem substantial, they are explicit and integrated into a coherent, math-

---

[10] The ideal level to raise the accession goals in the RRM tool to ensure at least 100 percent of the accession goal is achieved varies based on the size of the accession goal and can influence the overall cost level. For lower goals, this is generally not needed, as 100 percent of the accession goal is typically achieved. A starting point is 150 percent of the difference between the predicted accession level and the accession goal. For persistent accession shortfalls, consider reallocating training seats.

ematically based model that yields consistent results. Consequently, the RRM tool is a valuable addition to the suite of the Army's planning tools. The RRM tool can quickly inform Army planners and leaders regarding potential trade-offs in monthly recruiting resources, recruit eligibility, environment, and training seat vacancies over both short and long time periods.

CHAPTER SIX

Conclusions

Over the past five years, the U.S. Army has recruited between 57,000 and 69,000 enlisted soldiers each year. Its recruiting enterprise is the largest among the military services. At the same time, recent recruiting requirements have been considerably lower than some historical numbers. The Army recruited 80,000 soldiers per year from FY 2006 to FY 2008, and averaged 136,000 per year during the 1980s. While recent accession requirements have been lower, demand for quality recruits and the recruiting market have changed, with the unemployment rate well below 5 percent in FY 2017, and the percentage of high school diploma holders averaging above 95 percent over the last five years.

Recruiting is a complex process. Enlistment contracts must be signed months in advance of the enlistee starting Basic Combat Training, and some recruits cancel their contracts during this time period. The resources used to attract new recruits, such as recruiters, bonuses, and advertising, differ not only in their productivity but also in time elapsed between resource use and productive response. The Army spent on average $1.5 billion annually in 2016 dollars on recruiting resources (including recruiter compensation) from FY 2001 to FY 2014, and nearly $2.0 billion annually in FY 2008 and FY 2009.[1] Historically, the Army tightens recruit eligibility policies during good recruiting environments to increase the average quality of its recruits, while during

---

[1]   As noted earlier, recruiters, advertising, and enlistment bonuses offered to prospective recruits peaked in FY 2007–2008. Because bonuses are paid upon completion of IET—and for bonuses over $10,000, the remainder is paid out over the remainder of the recruit's term of enlistment—the actual costs incurred by the Army peaked in FY 2008–2009.

difficult recruiting conditions it relaxes eligibility policies to achieve its annual accession requirement. During difficult recruiting conditions, it has offered additional enlistment waivers, permitted more soldiers with prior service to enlist, and lowered educational and test score requirements.

Understanding how recruiting resources and enlistment eligibility policies work together as a system under varying recruiting requirements and environments is critical for decisionmakers who want to use their limited resources to efficiently and effectively achieve the Army's accession requirements. The RRM developed in this report considers the relationship among the monthly level and mix of recruiting resources, the recruiting environment, recruit eligibility policies, accumulated contracts, and training seat targets. It models how these factors combine to produce monthly accessions and the number of enlistment contracts at the fiscal year's end that are scheduled to access in the following fiscal year.

The RRM reflects the complex sequence of events leading to an accession. It consists of a contract production submodel, a DEP retention submodel, and a cost allocation submodel. The contract production submodel weighs the trade-offs between economic conditions and resources used to produce overall and HQ enlistment contracts (where HQ reflects the DoD standard of contracts where the enlistee has a formal high school diploma and scores in the upper fiftieth percentile of the AFQT). Based on the contract characteristics (e.g., HQ contract, quick-ship bonus) and training seat vacancies, contracts are scheduled to leave for basic training (i.e., access into the Army) at a specific time. The time between contract and accession is known as the time in the DEP. The DEP retention submodel captures the probabilistic cancellation of the enlistment contract over these months. The third submodel accounts for the resourcing costs that were paid in order to achieve the fiscal year's enlistment contracts and accessions.

The RRM by itself can only make predictions regarding whether a resourcing plan is sufficient to achieve an accession mission. To determine an efficient allocation of resources, we also develop an optimization algorithm. This algorithm is designed to find the cost-minimizing portfolio of recruiting resources conditional on the recruiting environment and Army-established recruit eligibility policies. It has three objectives: (1) produce enough accessions to fill each month's training seats; (2) achieve a target number of contracts in the DEP that are scheduled to access in the next fiscal year, also known as the entry pool; and (3) minimize total costs. We refer to the combination of the RRM and the optimization algorithm as the RRM tool.

We demonstrate using the RRM to analyze an accession goal for a specified resourcing plan, and provide six examples of how the RRM tool can be used to inform policymakers concerning potential resource and policy trade-offs, or how it can be used to prepare for alternative recruiting conditions or requirements. These examples include cost trade-offs based on

1. alternative recruiting environments
2. alternative resourcing strategies
3. alternative recruit eligibility policies
4. within-year goal or policy changes
5. five-year planning
6. alternative accession goals.

These examples demonstrate the versatility of the RRM tool for considering trade-offs across the recruiting enterprise. The RRM can provide resourcing alternatives to Army leadership that can achieve accession goals and potentially save hundreds of millions of dollars. Thus, it is a valuable addition to the suite of the Army's planning tools.

The examples provided in this report demonstrate important strategic-level trade-offs. As the difficulty level of recruiting changes in response to changes in accession requirements or changes in recruiting conditions, success and efficiency require different mixes and levels of recruiting resources and enlistment eligibility policies. In combination with recruiting environment predictions from the Recruiting Difficulty Index tool of Wenger et al. (forthcoming), Army planners can use the RRM tool to consider the potential cost and resourcing requirements for a range of recruiting contingencies. Our example of alternative resourcing strategies demonstrates that a strategy emphasizing one resource in lieu of other resources (e.g., bonuses when policymakers are reactive to a difficult recruiting environment rather than being proactive in planning for it) can be substantially more expensive than using a mix of resources. Additionally, we show that changing recruit eligibility policies can reduce recruiting resource costs substantially. When the RRM is used in combination with the Recruit Selection Tool (Orvis et al., forthcoming), policymakers can consider the first-term costs associated with broadening eligibility criteria in addition to the recruiting costs. Within-year analyses demonstrate the substantial cost savings and higher probability of goal achievement when resources are optimally adjusted to deal with changing accession requirements. The five-year planning example demonstrates how policymakers can use the RRM tool to determine efficient and effective resourcing and eligibility policies to meet long-range recruiting objectives and to weigh the desirability and feasibility of alternative objectives in supporting end-strength goals.

The RRM tool is not prescriptive. It informs Army planners and leaders regarding potential trade-offs in monthly recruiting resources conditional on recruit eligibility policies and the recruiting environment, over both short and long time periods. It does this through a coherent, mathematically based model that yields consistent results with explicit assumptions and caveats. Consequently, it represents a step forward in helping Army leaders shape a cost-efficient strategy capable of achieving the Army's accession requirements. The continued success of the RRM tool will require updating the model to reflect the current effectiveness of recruiting resources, and future enhancements could include integration with existing planning and budgeting models to make the RRM tool a budgeting resource in addition to a strategic resource.

Example of Changes in Production Elasticities

This appendix deals with a technical issue related to how measured elasticities on a production curve that exhibit diminishing or constant returns to an input could result in increasing or increasing then decreasing elasticities over a range of inputs. The source of this result is related to the relative change in the input compared with the output. Consider the two illustrative examples in Table A.1.

The first example reflects constant returns of output Y from a fixed increment of input X. The second example reflects diminishing returns of output Y from a fixed increment of input X. Recall that an elasticity is calculated as the percentage change in output Y divided by a percentage change in input X. The point elasticity at a point midway between input X_1 and X_2 (e.g., calculating the elasticity at 0.1 [midpoint] would use $X_1 = 0$ and $X_2 = 0.2$) is calculated numerically using the following midpoint formula:

$$\text{Elasticity} = \left(\frac{Y_2 - Y_1}{(Y_2 + Y_1)/2}\right) \Bigg/ \left(\frac{X_2 - X_1}{(X_2 + X_1)/2}\right)$$

where Y_1 corresponds to the output from X_1, and Y_2 corresponds to the output from X_2, all else equal. In both of these examples, the output Y starts from a relatively high level, suggesting that, while X has a positive impact in producing Y, it represents a small fraction of overall production. Consequently, as input X increases, the percentage

Table A.1
Illustration of Elasticity Calculation Under Alternative Assumptions

		Example 1: Constant Returns		
Input X	Output Y	Percentage Change in X	Percentage Change in Y	Elasticity
0.0	30,000			
0.1	30,930	2.00	0.06	0.03
0.2	31,860	1.00	0.06	0.06
0.3	32,790	0.67	0.06	0.09
0.4	33,720	0.50	0.06	0.11
0.5	34,650	0.40	0.05	0.13
0.6	35,580	0.33	0.05	0.16
0.7	36,510	0.29	0.05	0.18
0.8	37,440	0.25	0.05	0.20
0.9	38,370	0.22	0.05	0.22
1.0	39,300			
		Example 2: Diminishing Returns		
Input X	Output Y	Percentage Change in X	Percentage Change in Y	Elasticity
0.0	30,000			
0.1	33,000	2.00	0.15	0.08
0.2	35,000	1.00	0.10	0.10
0.3	36,500	0.67	0.07	0.10
0.4	37,500	0.50	0.05	0.09
0.5	38,250	0.40	0.03	0.08
0.6	38,750	0.33	0.02	0.06
0.7	39,000	0.29	0.01	0.03
0.8	39,125	0.25	0.01	0.02
0.9	39,225	0.22	0.00	0.02
1.0	39,300			

NOTE: The numbers provided in this table are illustrative.

change in Y is relatively small and diminishing, as represented in the fourth column. However, the dynamics of the elasticity measurement are driven by the sharp decrease in the percentage change in X. Analytically, if the output function is $Y = a + bX + cX^2$, then the elasticity becomes:

$$\text{Elasticity} = \frac{\partial Y}{\partial X} \cdot \frac{X}{Y} = \frac{bX + 2cX^2}{a + bX + cX^2}$$

If $c = 0$, then the production function exhibits constant returns. In this case, as bX grows relative to a, the elasticity converges toward one from below. If $c < 0$ as in the case of diminishing returns, then elasticity grows if X increases but will eventually decrease.

The increasing and decreasing nature of the elasticities reported in Chapter Four reflect the mechanical relationship derived here. The important takeaway for the purposes of this report is the range of potential elasticities. If the range of potential elasticities were outside what had been previously reported in the enlistment supply literature, then it would be notable. The results reported in Chapter Four, however, typically fall within ranges previously observed in the literature.

References

Accession Policy, "Accession Goals, Achievement and Quality," Office of the Under Secretary of Defense for Personnel and Readiness, 2017.

Asch, Beth, Paul Heaton, James Hosek, Paco Martorelli, Curtis Simon, and John Warner, *Cash Incentives and Military Enlistment, Attrition, and Reenlistment*, Santa Monica, Calif.: RAND Corporation, MG-950-OSD, 2010.

Asch, Beth, James Hosek, and John Warner, "New Economics of Manpower in the Post-Cold War Era," in Todd Sandler and Keith Harley, eds., *Handbook of Defense Economics*, Amsterdam, Netherlands: Elsevier, 2007, pp. 1076–1138.

Bureau of Labor Statistics, "Civilian Unemployment Rate: 16 Years and Over." As of April 5, 2018:
https://data.bls.gov/

Defense Manpower Data Center. As of April 5, 2018:
https://www.dmdc.osd.mil/appj/dwp/dwp_reports.jsp

Dertouzos, James N., *The Cost-Effectiveness of Military Advertising: Evidence from 2002–2004*, Santa Monica, Calif.: RAND Corporation, DB-565-OSD, 2009.

Dertouzos, James N., and Steven Garber, *Is Military Advertising Effective? An Estimation Methodology and Applications to Recruiting in the 1980s and 90s*, Santa Monica, Calif.: RAND Corporation, MR-1591-OSD, 2003.

———, *Human Resource Management and Army Recruiting: Analyses of Policy Options*, Santa Monica, Calif.: RAND Corporation, MG-433-A, 2006.

———, *Performance Evaluation and Army Recruiting*, Santa Monica, Calif.: RAND Corporation, MG-562-A, 2008.

Goldberg, Lawrence, Dennis D. Kimko, and Maggie X. Li, *Analysis and Forecasts of Army Enlistment Supply*, Alexandria, Va.: Institute for Defense Analyses, NS D-5466, 2015.

Joint Advertising Market Research and Studies, *The Target Population for Military Recruitment: Youth Eligible to Enlist Without a Waiver*, Monterey, Calif.: Defense Manpower Data Center, 2016.

Orvis, Bruce R., Steven Garber, Philip Hall-Partyka, Christopher Maerzluft, and Tiffany Tsai, *Recruiting Strategies to Support the Army's All-Volunteer Force*, Santa Monica, Calif.: RAND Corporation, RR-1211-A, 2016.

Orvis, Bruce R., Christopher E. Maerzluft, Sung-Bou Kim, Michael G. Shanley, and Heather Krull. *Prospective Outcome Assessment for Alternative Recruit Selection Policies*, Santa Monica, Calif.: RAND Corporation, forthcoming.

Polich, J. Michael, James N. Dertouzos, and S. James Press, *The Enlistment Bonus Experiment*, Santa Monica, Calif.: RAND Corporation, R-3353-FMP, 1986.

Warner, John, Curtis Simon, and Deborah Payne, *Enlistment Supply in the 1990's: A Study of the Navy College Fund and Other Enlistment Incentive Programs*, Washington, D.C.: Defense Manpower Data Center, DMDC Report No. 2000-015, 2001.

———, "The Military Recruiting Productivity Slowdown: The Roles of Resources, Opportunity Cost, and the Tastes in Youth," *Defence and Peace Economics*, Vol. 14, No. 5, 2003, pp. 329–342.

Wenger, Jeffrey, David Knapp, Bruce R. Orvis, and Tiffany Tsai, *Developing a National Recruiting Difficulty Index: A Multi-Equation Endogenous Regressor Approach*, Santa Monica, Calif.: RAND Corporation, forthcoming.